RECONNAISSANCE MAN

By Aaron Clarey

Copyright © 2016 by Aaron Clarey

All rights reserved. No part of this publication may be reproduced, distributed, or transmitted in any form or by any means, including photocopying, recording, or other electronic or mechanical methods, without the prior written permission of the publisher, except in the case of brief quotations embodied in critical reviews and certain other noncommercial uses permitted by copyright law.

To All the Agents in the Field who let me crash on their couches

TABLE OF CONTENTS

Who Should Read This Book — 7

PART 1 - Philosophy
Introduction — 10
Chapter 1 - Cart Before the Horse — 16
Chapter 2 - What is Reconnaissance? — 34

PART 2 – Practicum
Chapter 3 – Logistics, Finance, & Education — 59
Chapter 4 – Psychological Hurdles — 115
Chapter 5 – Familial Hurdles — 130
Chapter 6 – Where to Recon — 140

WHO SHOULD READ THIS BOOK

Like many of my previous books, the younger a person reads "Reconnaissance Man" the more help it will provide in life. Ideally, one would read this book at the age of 14 and start laying the groundwork to become a Reconnaissance Man as early as possible. However, we all know life isn't "ideal" and millions of men and women, of all ages, face the problems this book intends to fix. Thus, there are three main groups of people, of varying ages, this book aims to help out.

The first are the 14-18 year olds who, if they play their cards right today, will have infinitely easier lives tomorrow. Again, this is the ideal scenario where a young man or woman would have the foresight to read this book, implement its recommendations, and enjoy lives the rest of us could only dream of having. Of course, most 14 year olds are not mature or wise enough to heed such advice, but it still doesn't change the fact that in the perfect world this book would be read before one becomes an adult.

The second group of people are college-aged and 20-somethings who are currently wandering the desert, trying to figure out who they are and what they want out of life. They are either attending college or recently-graduated, but still have no idea what they want to do in life, or worse, they graduated from college and their dreams they worked so hard for are not materializing. This book aims to explain why life is not going the way it was supposed to, and provides a clear and outlined path to a reality-based life that ensures you won't waste your entire future chasing dreams that will never come true.

The third group are those 30 and older who, unfortunately, wasted their lives chasing dreams that were never going to come true. They went to college. They followed their hearts hoping the money would follow. They did everything they were told to do, and now have absolutely nothing to show for it. If you're under 50, perhaps this book may provide some last minute salvation, allowing you to salvage what remains of your life. But for the rest, it at least explains why life didn't go the way you were promised. And at least that provides a little bit of serenity and sanity you didn't have before.

PART I
PHILOSOPHY

INTRODUCTION

Without a doubt, the single worst decision I ever made in my life was to move to Minnesota. Of course, at the time it didn't seem to be a mistake. Matter of fact, given the information I had at the time, it was the wisest choice I could make. My fondest memories were from Minnesota where I fished with my grandpa, played with my aunt, and was spoiled by my grandma. People in Minnesota were always nice, helping my family out when we needed it. It had reciprocity with my home state (Wisconsin) which would make college tuition cheaper. And it was just far enough away from my parents that I'd be "independent," but not so far away I couldn't return home to visit. In all honesty it was a no-brainer, so in 1993 I moved out and attended the University of Minnesota. But the decision to move to Minnesota set forth a chain of events that would limit, control, and cripple the amount of happiness and success I'd have in my life. And 23 years later the consequences of that ill-fated decision still limit and affect my life today.

In moving to Minnesota, consciously or not, I had planted roots in the state and its culture. These roots manifested themselves in the form of social networks, connections, contacts, relationships, and a career that would support and sustain my life. However, the drawbacks of planting roots in any one place is that you are indeed "rooted" to that area. And no matter how bad the soil, to uproot, move, and start anew is costly and inefficient as you essentially have to start all over again. This results in a trap where, even though your hometown may not be terribly kind, perhaps even outright hostile against you, it's still better than abandoning the various social and career networks you formed as those networks are efficient and sustain your life (ask yourself why Baghdad still has a population of 7.2 million or Jews stayed in Germany to the point they were being put in cattle cars). And so, unknowingly, at the naïve age of 18 I anchored myself to Minnesota and committed to the culture therein.

Unfortunately, Minnesota sucks.

While my favorite memories in life were from Minnesota, they were not the product of being in Minnesota. They were a function of being with my grandpa and other loving people. Fishing, getting ice cream, playing with wind-up toy airplanes, these memories were 100% due to the people around me, not the state of Minnesota. The reality, unfortunately, is that Minnesotans are some of the coldest, fakest, phoniest people in the United States. So much so that reciprocity-seeking college students from Wisconsin call it "Minnesota Ice," not "Minnesota Nice."

Another factor that skewed my opinion of Minnesota was that my visits there were during summer vacation…not winter. Hanging out with grandpa, fishing from a bridge, with root beer in hand is one of the greatest things a young boy will ever enjoy in Minnesota…in July. But if you're unlucky enough to be a security guard on the University of Minnesota campus in January (and I was) you get to patrol in -30°F temperatures, deal with anti-freeze freezing, water pipes bursting, and going without the sun for two full months. It is a constant fight against nature to stay alive, and though fun for a child to have a "snow day," as an adult it drains your psyche.

And then there's the taxes.

No kid having a root beer float with his grandpa contemplates the tax rates at the state and municipal levels. He doesn't look up property taxes, nor considers income tax brackets. And he doesn't ask about the consequences of the state's pro-Somali immigration policy. But if you were naïve enough to plant roots here as a college student and establish what career you could on its rocky soil, you'll soon find you're in the 6th highest-taxed state, the only state that didn't vote for Ronald Reagan in 1984, and a state that LOATHES successful, hard-working people.

If you have the slightest inkling to be successful, to have any modicum of financial success, or you simply have an ounce of self-respect, you are an idiot for living here. But that point may ultimately be moot if you met the love of your life in college, got married and had kids, bought yourself a house, and inextricably rooted yourself in socialist Minnesota via a mortgage, a family, a career, not to mention, precious little Timmy just *HAVING TO* attend the same school as his friends. Alas, you're stuck here not only with the punishing weather and fake people, but you get to pay egregious taxes on top of it.

I could go on, but these cumulative traits (the people, the weather, and the taxes) are all key determinants of the amount of happiness, success, accomplishment, and freedom you will enjoy in the environment you live. And while you'd think people would assess these things before moving to a town, going off to college, or taking a job out of state, the truth is factors and forces within our lives (that have nothing to do with the aforementioned variables) determine where we choose to live. Sadly, the result is we live lives that are condemned to be a mere fraction of their potential.

The truth is I should not be writing this book in my crappy duplex in White Bear Lake, Minnesota.
I should be writing it from my swank patio that overlooks Rapid City, South Dakota.

I should not have attended college at the University of Minnesota where I endured harsh winters and cold people.
I should have gone to school in Colorado where I could hike, bike, spelunk, and kayak with fun, adventurous friends.

And I should not have a mortgage on this house.
I should have never bought a house in the first place, opting instead for cheap bachelor pads that would allow me to come and go as I please.

And no doubt you also have your own personal regrets.

The only problem is that's living in "Shoulda Land."

With hindsight being 20/20 we can all regretfully point to the erroneous decisions we made in life and say, *"If I had only done this, then I'd be immeasurably better off now!"* However, whereas wishing to go back in time to make different decisions is impossible, it is possible to fundamentally change the way we make these vital and early life decisions that determine so much of our future. However, in order to do this you have to abandon conventional wisdom. You have to stop telling yourself you need to go to college immediately after high school. You have to stop thinking life's opportunities are limited to your hometown or state. And you have to stop looking to everybody else for guidance as to what you should be doing individually.

In short, you have to dedicate the time, effort, and energy it takes to explore this country and yourself in order to find which environment offers you the most opportunity, and thus the best shot at living a great life.

And in order to do that you have to become a Reconnaissance Man.

CHAPTER 1
CART BEFORE THE HORSE

We're Doing It Wrong

Conventional wisdom since time immemorial has been that upon graduating from high school you IMMEDIATELY go to college. This then commits you to a life-long career which will serve as the sole economic engine that will support and finance you for your entire life. You're then to buy a house as soon as possible to "save on rent," while also contemplating grad school as that will certainly advance your career. While juggling all of this, add a spouse and the inevitable children that come with it into the mix. Sock away for your 401k or IRA. Put in your 30 years. Retire at 65. Collect social security, and then die surrounded by children and grandchildren you have yet to name. This is the plan. This is the route. This is the script our elders have deemed is in your best interests. This why you have had this advice pounded into your skull ever since you were a little child.

And all of it is flawed.

Not that going to college is a bad idea or a grad degree won't necessarily increase your salary. Nor is buying a house a bad idea or saving for retirement. But this "time tested advice" is flawed not only because it is impossible to apply a universal "life plan" to 300 million unique American individuals, but because mandating everybody go to college is just plain wrong and by chronological default screws up the remainder of advice, rendering all of it moot:

After graduating from high school you must IMMEDIATELY go to college.

It is this advice that has ruined the lives of two full generations of Americans and Westerners.

Perhaps at some point in American history it paid to immediately attend college. It boosted your lifetime earnings, dramatically increased your chances of finding employment, and otherwise proved to be a huge net benefit to your life. But times have changed and with nearly everybody going to college (not to mention economic growth being halved) an education bubble has formed where students now graduate with worthless degrees, poor job prospects, and insurmountable debts that will crush and cripple them for the rest of their financial lives. But economic reasons aside, there are other reasons why going to college immediately after high school is not only wrong, but absolutely damaging to a young person's future. And these reasons are based in just plain, simple logic.

First, it is laughable that a 17 year old junior (which is the age one must start applying to colleges and determine a major) has the wisdom, experience, and self-knowledge to choose a major that will become their life-long career and passion. They've never worked a real job. They've never supported themselves in the real world. And their entire lives have been in the context of childhood, not adulthood. They simply haven't lived long enough to develop a knowledge about the world (let alone themselves) to see what kind of role or capacity they should play in it.

Second, school is a mental prison, especially for the intelligent who are presumably college-bound. While you would think school would prepare a young person to make a wise decision about what to study, the truth is school puts most kids' brains into comas. School is not a place young people look forward to attending where they'll be intellectually stimulated, mentally invigorated, leading them towards new epiphanies and self-discovery. Schools are mental torture facilities that we force our children to attend because we don't want to raise them or educate them at home. So, while one would think a high school junior would know what they'd want to do after 13 years of school, the truth is most students go into a state of arrested development and are just as prepared to make major life decisions at 16 as they were when they first attended kindergarten.

Third, depending on which statistics you want to use, about half of college graduates don't end up working in their field. Worse, even if they work in their field, they rarely stay there as the average person changes careers about five times over the course of a lifetime. This not only calls into question the entire point of going to college, but completely debunks the premise that college should be your first and most urgent step after high school.

And finally, there's underemployment. Again the statistics will vary, but anywhere between 20% and 50% of college graduates are working jobs that are beneath their skill level and education. Though more of a problem Gen X and Millennials face, it behooves the question, *"Why go to college if you're only going to get a job you could have done when you were in the 9th grade?"*

When you sum this up, young people face an impossible task. We tell them their only shot at success in life is through college. But not only is college becoming increasingly expensive, it is also becoming increasingly worthless. They have to risk *four years of youth and tens of thousands of dollars* on a bet whose odds are worsening.

But if this decision wasn't hard enough, it gets even worse.

They're so young they:

1. Don't know what they want to do
2. Don't know where they want to live
3. Don't know who they are

And

4. Lack the real world experience necessary to answer these three vital and very important questions.

Without knowing the answers to these important questions, how can a young person possibly make an informed and wise decision about something as important as their future? It is almost a guarantee they will make the wrong decision, waste four years of their youth, and cripple their financial futures with student loans.

Still, we browbeat it into their heads that they "must go to college" and that "the key to success is college." Some parents I know go so far as to threaten to kick their children out of the house if they choose to work instead of go to college. And thus, like forcing 18 year old draftees into the trenches of WWI, they go cluelessly and helplessly, but most assuredly to pay the dear price of an impaired and crippled future. All because we forced them to go about life the wrong way.

The Price You Pay for Doing It the Wrong Way

Dave was one of only two bosses I both liked and respected in my banking career. He was blunt and direct, but also fair. After turning in my two weeks' notice, Dave thought it was his place to give me some wise career advice. By this time I was 36, knew full well what I was doing, and only viewed working at this particular bank to make enough money so I could pay down and refinance my mortgage. But even though I had no intention of ever returning to banking ever again he said,

"You're not cut out for banking. Banking just isn't for you. Go write, go ride your motorcycle, go teach dance or something. But banking just isn't for you."

While I knew he was right, I wish I had gotten that advice when I was 16 and not 36. It would have saved me an incalculable price. It would have spared me the 20 years of time, youth, expense, and mental strife I wasted in finance. It would have resulted in a much better, happier, and productive life. I'd likely have a more intellectually challenging and rewarding career. Certainly an increased life expectancy. And I'd wager a much better chance of sitting on my theoretical patio in Rapid City. Ironically (perhaps, tragically), I received this bit of advice only after it took me 20 years to deduce it for myself. I wanted to say to Dave *"Now you tell me."*

But this dark humor aside, there is a very important moral to the story. I paid an egregious price for following the advice of my elders and immediately attending college. And if we tally up the costs, the price is staggering:

- 4 years of college
- $20,000 in tuition
- 4 years of late night studying and not having fun
- 4 years of working while going to school fulltime
- 18 years (including internships) trying to make it in finance
- No traveling or partying
- Never having job security
- And all of the mental strife that comes with such a lifestyle

In short, I effectively **wasted my entire youth** pursuing a dream that was never meant to be. And this says nothing of "what could have been" had I received Dave's advice when I was 16 and chose another path. Sadly, however, my experience is not unique, but quite universal in that nearly everyone today in America has wasted what I estimate to be AT MINIMUM 10 years of their youth and money simply because they did life the wrong way. And while it is impossible to tally and quantify the price we've all individually paid, we can summarize the price future generations will pay if they continue to repeat our mistakes.

First, and perhaps most costly, is your wasted time and youth. You are only young once and while you have the physique, life, vigor, and energy it should be spent pursuing life's greatest joys, not buried in books for prerequisite classes you'll never use. Sadly, all of us are mandated to waste 13 years of our youth in the K-12 system, but once "free" we just mindlessly plug ourselves right back into the education matrix…but this time paying for it with tuition. It isn't until we're about 24 do we truly get free from the education system. But, again, unless we took the time to sit down and really think about what we wanted to study in college, it's almost a guarantee an entire quarter century of our life was wasted on an education we'll never use.

Talk to anybody in their 30's, 40's, or 50's and you'll find they're not only unlikely to be using their degree or education, but are somehow either still in school, training themselves in some other field, or have just given up and are now working a job to simply put food on the table. College and their education have very little to do with their lives and was largely the single most expensive waste of their youth. And I guarantee you the majority of them would recommend you become a ski bum, a vagabond, or a world traveler before you waste four years in college. In short, unless you are one of the incredibly rare 17 year olds who knows precisely what they want to do for a living, it is almost a 100% guarantee you will pay the unaffordable price of four to six years of your youth to a bunch of hacks posing as professors.

Second are the financial costs.

One of my favorite debates to get into is with somebody who thinks there's value to a college education beyond the increased wages it can command in the labor market. They say things like "you can't put a price on education" or "any degree is a good degree" as they typically try to rationalize why they blew $100,000 on their "Masters in Portuguese Sociological Lesbian 16th Century Unicorn Sculpture Studies."

The reason I find the debate so entertaining, however, is because of the price tag colleges are demanding for their degrees. Today (2016) the average cost of a public school degree is $24,000 A YEAR while a private school costs $48,000 A YEAR.

That's nearly a $100,000 investment for a public school degree and $200,000 for a private one. You could practically buy a house for cash with that kind of money, but somehow we're supposed to ignore that price tag according to the cheerleaders for higher education, as we blindly just "follow our hearts because the money will follow."

But step back, clear your eyes, (and more importantly) get your head out of your ass and just think about it for a second.

At the age of 17 you're being asked to:

1. Commit to spend $100,000-$200,000 on just a BACHELORS degree
2. Borrow the vast majority of that sum which you will unlikely ever be able to pay back
3. And not worry about what kind of degree it is or what its earnings prospects are because…

….well, choose any excuse people give:

"You can't put a price on education."
"It's worth the college experience."
"Follow your heart and the money will follow."
"Any degree is a good degree."

"We'll cut you off if you don't go to school."

Any sober, realistic assessment of this proposition will conclude it is a losing one. It is, frankly, insane to invest/borrow this much money on an education you are just not sure of and one you're statistically unlikely to use in your future. Worse, the price tag of a college degree is the least of your problems. The consequential student debts that are incurred paying for college haunt and cripple college graduates well into their 30's, sometimes their 40's, prohibiting them from living normal lives. Today's millennials, saddled with student loans, can't afford homes, fewer can afford families, and it's all because they "just had to go to college." This then leads to the third, and arguably, most dramatic cost – opportunity costs.

Revisiting the world of "Shoulda Land," ask yourself what you could've done had you postponed college, took the time to find yourself, figure out life, and then went to school for a degree that would not only pay, but one that you would have an interest in. It may not guarantee the world's greatest job or riches or wealth, but you would likely be immeasurably better off than you are today.

I would indeed have that house in Rapid City with that patio, a degree in geology, working the oil fields, coal mines, and gold mines out west, all while hiking the mountains in my back yard... that's if I wasn't road-tripping on my motorcycle into Colorado for fossil hunting and gold panning.

You wouldn't be stuck in that soul-sucking cubicle job, running TPS reports, hating every minute of it, but needing it because you took a mortgage out on a McMansion&Wife™ you could barely afford. You'd have majored in computer programming, gone out to Thailand, and then been working remotely from a beach as an IT consultant from Phuket, all while sipping on 50 cent mojitos.

And you wouldn't be a miserable, barely employed 48 year old adjunct professor teaching "Intro to Women's Studies" as you beg for grant money to pay off your master's degree. You'd be a stay at home mom with a husband and three loving children who also runs a small accounting business online with her CPA.

In immediately going to college, as well as planting your roots in an area that is merely convenient, you almost guarantee you'll be:

Living in an area you don't want to.
Working a job you hate.
Constantly pining to do something else, elsewhere. While tragically not even knowing what else is out there, so you don't even know what you're missing out on in the first place.

But perhaps the worst opportunity cost of doing life the wrong way is when you finally figure out what you want out of life, but then have to embark on the journey to get there before you die. The investment banker who realized he just wanted to fish, but dies of a stroke because of all the stress. Or the "strong, independent feminist" who got her doctorate in social work to manage that prestigious non-profit, but at a post-menopausal 52 realized all she wanted was a family and kids. These unrecoverable life regrets are the true price we pay when we mindlessly embark down the path our foolish elders told us to.

Finally, there are the mental costs associated with all of the above.

The first and arguably most taxing mental price you pay is when the life and dreams you were promised by your elders are crushed by merciless reality. One second you're about to graduate from college with honors, replete with a $60,000 a year job offer right around the corner, the next you're slinging coffee for $8/hr realizing it will be 50 years before you pay off your student loans. But what makes it worse is that nobody tells you why life didn't turn out the way you were promised. The sheer amount of lies and propaganda you were told from K thru college were not only told to keep you ignorantly naïve in a bubble, but also to suck as much financial resources out of you before dumping your insolvent corpse into the real world. And once the education industry got all they could out of you, they have no reason to keep you around, let alone explain to you how the real world actually works. This then results in a period of several years, perhaps even decades of "wandering in the desert" where young 20 somethings try to reconcile what they've been told their entire lives with the contradicting reality that's brutally punching them in their face. Some finally wake up and start to accept reality for what it is. Others remain delusional and hate-filled their entire lives.

This parlays into a second mental price people pay – living a delusional life. After 25 years of bad advice and propaganda, it's hard for the human brain to just "flip a switch" and say, *"Oh, what I've been told this entire time is just simply wrong? Up until now my life has been an entire lie?? Cool, easy peasy! I'll just change my entire life outlook correspondingly!"* People will still think there's something wrong with them, that they're having bad luck, or they're somehow completely missing something. They will never question that there's something wrong with the system itself. And therefore, like me, they keep plodding along in a career that just wasn't meant for them, wasting decades pursuing a delusional life. This conflict between the individual's pre-conditioning and reality results in friction that takes an immense mental toll.

One person I knew always wanted to be a teacher when he was in high school, only to spend 20 years in teaching hating every second of it until he (once again) died of a stroke. I myself spent nearly two decades in banking thinking my ability to predict markets, bubbles, and assess market risk would be appreciated, only to constantly ram heads with management as they approved every loan, sold them off to dupes, while collecting commission and fees on those bad loans. And I know more than one career-obsessed woman who swallowed whole the "stay at home moms are losers" motif who now, in their 40's, regret not having children. I could go on, but one cannot simply undo 25 years of mental conditioning overnight, and it is a guarantee a mental price will be paid as you try to reconcile this programming with reality.

And then there's the anger and rage.

When you finally realize just how much you were lied to about the real world, intentionally or not, you cannot help but go into full-blown anger, rage, and often depression as you realize just how much of your one, precious, short, and finite life was wasted. Be it the doctoral candidate who realizes his degree in English will get him nowhere or the nerd who realizes being the nice guy lands you no girls, you cannot help but get angry as the world has robbed you of the most valuable thing in your life – your youth. There is no solution as there's no way you can get it back. So despair sets in, you become bitter, perhaps even depressed and only the strongest shake themselves out of it to salvage what remains of their life. But most turn into shells of their former, happy, idealistic youthful selves, ironically lessening what life they have left.

When you tally these costs up – the time, the youth, the money, the opportunity costs, and the mental strife – it is just too steep a price to pay for any individual. The fear that you'll "fall behind" if you dare to take a couple years off to "figure things out" is unfounded as those two years are a fraction of the decades of life and thousands of dollars you'll waste otherwise. Those two years spent "figuring things out" are nothing compared to the decades of mental strife, suffering, and pain you'll endure if you rush off, hastily committing to a degree you're not too sure of. And those two years are literally life-savers as they can mean the difference between living the dream, or dreaming of a life you're never going to have.

Those two years are called "reconnaissance."

CHAPTER 2
WHAT IS RECONNAISSANCE?

"Answer Me These Questions Three"

There are no hard and fast rules to conducting reconnaissance or becoming a Reconnaissance Man. Truth be told, becoming a "Reconnaissance Man" is a completely new idea and is simply the advice I'd give to my younger self were I to do it all over again. However, while this is all new ground yet to be fully explored, experimented with, and discovered, you can't conduct reconnaissance in a disorganized and slipshod manner. Some structure, logic, and discipline is required to be successful, otherwise you're just another 36 year old ski bum in Colorado, getting high on pot, claiming you're "*Still discovering yourself maaaan!*" To this end, we need to understand what the goal of reconnaissance is and what's required of us to achieve that goal.

In short, the goal of becoming a Reconnaissance Man is to lay the foundation of your future life ***as early and accurately as possible*** so you do not waste it like most of us did. Find out what it is you truly want to do in life, what you want to be when you grow up, what you want to achieve before you die, and what kind of a person you'd like to become along the way. It's what we're all trying to figure out, but instead of following the flawed conventional wisdom that has ruined the lives of millions, becoming a Reconnaissance Man aims to be much more efficient and effective. It aims to answer these questions ***early as possible in life, not when it's too late or a significant percentage of your life is already over***. To do this, every person needs to answer three vital and important questions:

1. Who am I?
2. What do I want to do?
3. Where do I want to live?

If you cannot answer these three questions then there's absolutely no reason for you to go to college, let alone make any other long term investments in your life. You simply lack the knowledge about yourself and the real world for your decisions to be effective. And, in reality, the vast majority of high school graduates, even 20 and 30 somethings, can't answer these questions. Therefore, any major decisions or long term plans made about your life are practically guaranteed to fail because you are operating from premises you just aren't sure of.

Therefore, the primary goal of becoming a Reconnaissance Man is to answer these three questions so a person can make wise AND EFFECTIVE decisions as to how to plot, plan, invest, and succeed in life.

"How do I answer these questions?"

If we were to list those three questions in order of importance, they would be pretty much in the exact same order they're in now.

"Who am I?" is obviously the most important question to answer because not only is it very personal to us, but it defines us, what we believe, and speaks directly to our sentience.

"What do I want to do?" is a logical close second because it also directly speaks to who we are, as well as what we want out of life.

"Where do I want to live?" seems a distant third. Some would even argue it isn't that important of a question at all. Matter of fact, there are many other questions you'd no doubt prefer answered, but out of the three it is last in terms of importance.

The problem, however, in organizing these questions in terms of importance is that it is theoretical, not practical.

Yes, to attain self-knowledge and self-discovery is likely the most important goal of every human being. And yes, to know what you should do in life is just about as important as the first question. But in order to answer these two very important life questions, we actually have to answer these questions in reverse. And the reason why is questions #1 and #2 cannot be answered until we answer #3. Ergo, when it comes to becoming a Reconnaissance Man we have to answer them in this order:

1. Where do I want to live?
2. What do I want to do?
3. Who am I?

The logic is very simple.

You, as an individual, do not exist in a vacuum in outer space, unaffected by the nothingness around you. If you did, there would be nothing to say about you for you would have nothing to interact with, reference from, or compare to. You would have no interaction with other people, having no meaningful conversations, observations, or epiphanies. You wouldn't even be able to make your mark on the planet via a legacy of art, literature, music, or innovation. In other words, answering the all-important question of *"Who am I?"* requires you exist in an environment of some kind in the first place. It is your environment and the people around you who define who you are. And these things not only define you, but give you meaning and purpose in life.

However, that is only one side of the equation. ***How you interact with them ALSO defines you***. Are you honest or a liar? Do you work hard or do you collect welfare? Are you capable of altruism and selflessness, or are you greedy and use people? Do you abide by realty or pout if you don't get your way? All these choices equally determine who you are just as much as the people and environment that surround you. Thus, the answer to *"Who am I?"* is a combination of how people and the environment interact with you and how you in turn interact with them.

But here is where traditional wisdom fails and being a Reconnaissance Man begins. Whereas the vast majority of effort, advice, and wisdom focuses on how you interact with your environment, rarely is the question brought up, "*What if we control the environment we're in?*" This is normally a laughable question because people just assume you don't control your environment or other people. And they're right. You don't. But while you can't control other people or the environment, you can CHOOSE which environment and people you interact with. And that is why the question, *"Where do I want to live?"* needs to be answered first because where you live determines your environment, the people in your life, and ultimately...

who you are.

Yes, Where You Live is That Important

While many people may disagree, if you think about it, where you live is that important. Simply because it affects, if not outright determines, so many things about your future.

We've discussed two of these aspects already. First, is how the roots you put down in any given area will have a tendency to keep you there. They will not only support and sustain your life, but create efficiencies and networks that will be increasingly difficult to remove yourself from, even if that environment grows hostile or even dangerous to you. Second, is how your environment ultimately determines and defines you because you simply have no other choice. It's the environment you're in and you get to live in/react to it no matter what you'd prefer. But there is so much more that is determined by where you live.

Fun for instance.

Have you ever met someone from Denver, Colorado?
Do you ever see them frown or scowl?
Do they ever seem sad or depressed?
Additionally, have you ever seen an obese person from Colorado?

No, they're all happy, sexy, smiley people, every one of them in shape having the time of their lives!

Why?

Because they live in arguably the coolest, most fun state ever – Colorado.

Mountain climbing, hiking, fossil hunting, kayaking, whitewater rafting, camping, biking, swimming, hang-gliding, micro-brewing, cliff jumping, gun-shooting, motorcycling, spelunking, skiing, snowboarding, race car driving, fishing, gold-panning, all with in-shape, athletic sexy people to boot!

Why would a young man, let alone anyone, go to college in uncultured, boring crap-holes like Minnesota, Ohio, Illinois, Iowa, New York, Alabama, etc., when you can go and live the dream in Colorado?

Closely related to fun is both physical and mental health.

If you choose the right area, you're not stuck indoors in Minnesota because it's -30°F outside. Nor are you stuck in traffic because it's LA. Nor are you stuck inside because it's 2AM in Chiraq. You're out hiking in 70 degree weather in the Black Hills of South Dakota. Running that 10 mile route you love in Washington State. Kayaking the Clark River in Missoula, Montana. Or riding your bike in Colorado Monument National Park in Grand Junction. Not only will choosing the right area prompt you to participate in hobbies, improving your physical health, they will also be passions, improving your mental state as well.

Even your chances of finding lifelong love is improved by choosing the right place to live as you will likely find like-minded people with similar passions and interests. Every hiking couple I know met through hiking. Every volleyball couple I know met through volleyball. And every ballroom dance couple I know met through ballroom dancing. You're not going to find your future husband with your shared passion for snowmobiling in Arizona, just as you're not going to find your future wife with your shared passion for mountain climbing in Mississippi. You need to go and live your life, live your dream, doing what you want, where you want, and you'll DRAMATICALLY increase your chances of finding a like-minded soulmate.

We could go on about all the other benefits that come from choosing a place wisely - employment opportunities, low crime, weather, everything. But all these reasons aside, there are frankly two compelling, more practical reasons why where you live is the most important question to answer. First, "who am I" and "what do I want to do" really can't be answered until you explore this country (perhaps the world) and find your place in it. No 17 year old kid is introspective enough to deeply ponder his or her existence to the point they know who they truly are. And most people (young or old) have not traveled the country enough to have the context and knowledge needed to know where to plant their roots. In short, it's futile trying to find out who you are and what you should do without first thoroughly exploring this country and what it has to offer you. Second, as it just so happens, the majority of people can't answer those first two vital and important questions anyway. Most people don't know who they are and most people don't know what they should do. Which makes *"Where should I live?"* the only question that can be answered in the here and now.

Because of this, becoming a Reconnaissance Man focuses solely on finding out where you should live before you do anything else. It aims to find out where in the United States you ultimately belong. And if you can determine that, you can determine everything else in life.

Putting It Into Practice

While a more thorough and detailed explanation of how to conduct reconnaissance will be covered in part two of this guide, it helps to have a bird's eye view to understand the general philosophy and strategy of becoming a Reconnaissance Man.

The operating principle behind being a Reconnaissance Man is that he or she KNOWS they can't move forward in life until they know what they want to do. They are also more than willing to spend two, three, even ten years wandering the desert answering that question because the alternative is infinitely more costly. To that end, they realize investing 2-5 years in reconnaissance today can save themselves decades of time and hundreds of thousands of dollars over the course of their life. And since the paramount goal of reconnaissance is to find out where you should live, an organized plan to thoroughly, yet efficiently explore the United States is required. That plan has three basic stages.

Stage One – Surveying the United States

The United States is huge. Only Canada and Russia are larger, but they have populations that are much smaller, meaning there's a lot more towns, cultures, and cities to explore in the US. You simply will not be able to do a thorough exploration of the country in a summer, let alone a year. So the first thing you have to do is just "get a feel" for the country.

This "get a feel" or surveying of the US is basically a mad-dash, rocket run road trip all across the country hitting every major city, major landmark, and national park in states you have an interest in. Your goal is not to find a city or town to fall in love with, but to find out which parts of the country you absolutely do NOT want to live in.

For example many people picture Wyoming as mountainous and beautiful, which it is…where there's mountains. The majority of the state is dry, desert prairie with rattlesnakes, brown recluse spiders, and the occasional gun-toting meth head. But you wouldn't know that until you actually drive through Wyoming and see it yourself.

Another example, a friend of mine from Wyoming hates Minnesota. Not because of the cold or taxes, but because of the trees. He feels claustrophobic in Minnesota because he's used to being able to see 30 miles over Wyoming's treeless rolling prairie, while in Minnesota you are constantly surrounded by trees. Odd eccentricities like this, which are unique to every individual, are enough to make a town, city, or state unviable as a place for you to live (pay special attention to allergies).

The point is, you should simply drive across the country, perhaps spending a day or two in major metro areas, just to get an idea of what you do and do not like.

You might like mountains. Then try Colorado.
You might not like people. Then try North Dakota.
You might like salsa dancing. Then try Miami.
You might like quiet. Then try Van Horn, Texas.

Just keep a keen eye out for what piques your interest and what definitely drives you away.

Stage Two – Focus

After surveying the land, you'll want to come up with a list of your top 10 or so places you found most promising and explore those further. This means spending a couple weeks in each town, getting to know the culture and routine of the people, as well as exploring the surrounding area to get an idea of whether or not this town is for you. The goal here is to find any deal breakers that would disqualify an area, usually deal breakers you haven't thought of or anticipated. For example, you may have fallen in love with the mountains, but the lack of cell phone coverage might be an issue. You might like fishing in the local lake, but the town might have slow internet speeds. Or you had a great time at that guy's house party drinking some homemade moonshine…only to find out it's because you were in a dry county. These drawbacks will become very apparent during a 14 day stay.

Stage Three – Trial Run

After living in a dozen towns for a couple weeks each, you will start to have a pretty good idea of what you do and do not like about different areas. Out of that list, you should have a top three or four candidates for your future hometown. Even though you may have lived there for two weeks, that still isn't enough time to thoroughly vet it. Novelty wears off and you still have to be in love with the place when it does. This requires living in those areas for three months, even a full year because different towns can drastically change with the seasons. You don't have to commit to three months because once you find out you don't like the place, you can scratch it off the list. But just like dating somebody, it's going to take about three months to really get to know that town. Hopefully, you find one that makes for the perfect hometown.

These stages do not have to be followed to the letter and are merely recommendations. You can certainly tweak the strategy by living in a major metro (say Seattle) and using that as a hub to explore other areas nearby (Yakima, Spokane, Portland, Vancouver, etc.). You could also become a vagabond roaming around aimlessly until you find a place you consider home. The larger point, however, is to employ some kind of screening process where you get to take in the entirety of the United States and then methodically whittle down your options. However, keep in mind this process can AND WILL take years. In my unplanned, unintentional, and completely accidental journey to become a Reconnaissance Man, it took me over 10 years to fully explore the US. I'm simply trying to provide a much more efficient method.

The Benefits of Reconnaissance

Assuming you do your reconnaissance correctly and adhere to some level of discipline and structure, chances are you will be well ahead of your peers in the game of life. The benefits to seriously contemplating your life, finding your place in it, and then taking a very logical approach to living it will not only sidestep major life mistakes, but pay huge dividends. But while the benefits of being a Reconnaissance Man are both immeasurable and innumerable you can expect to see concrete results in the following areas of your life.

Financial

In not blindly rushing off to college you will avoid the single largest problem plaguing modern day millennials – college debt. This, of course, assumes you're working in the meantime, building up a war chest to finance an education once you've figured out what you'd like to study. But in insisting you first find out what you want to do in life before committing to a college education you will not only ensure you don't waste it, but will lessen your reliance on student loans. This simple fact will put you ahead of your peers by years, perhaps even decades as you are neither hindered nor crippled by $100,000 in student loans and a worthless degree that offers no hope of being able to pay them off.

Further financial benefits will cascade from this exercise in patience, most notably a better career. In choosing your education wisely, you will likely benefit from more reliable and stable employment.

You'll like your job more which means you'll not only work harder, but stand better chances for promotion, raises, and advancement. Over the course of time, this, combined with a lack of student debt, will dramatically improve your personal finances allowing you to buy a house, raise a family, or perhaps just travel and enjoy life while most of your peers are still slinging coffee to pay off their Masters in Baboon Herbal Medicine Yoga Latino Studies.

Finally, while they say "money isn't everything," it sure as hell makes life a lot easier. Being poor and lacking job security sucks. It prevents you from enjoying life and takes a drastic toll on your mental health. This then affects other aspects of life including friendships and even your family. It's no coincidence that "finances" are the #1 reason cited for marital problems. And if you think you were having financial problems before, just wait until you get divorced. This doesn't mean becoming a Reconnaissance Man will vaccinate you against divorce, but the financial stability that comes with it lessens a whole host of problems tangentially related to personal finances.

Time

As it stands right now, the majority of Americans, both young and old, waste or have wasted their lives in three major categories.

One, they waste years in school either aimlessly floating from one degree to the next, never settling on one, or they blow 4-8 years on a completely worthless degree that will never pay off. Since neither approach results in employment, most people who waste their time in college are inevitably forced to go back, spending an additional 2-4 years getting an education that actually has a career attached to the end of it. I don't know how many people I knew in the 90's who proudly defended their humanities degrees, only to now be in their 40's sheepishly having to attend some two year program to stand at least a chance of retiring before they die. Regardless, the point is you don't want to be a 45 year old loser, "going back to school" to get a degree that finally pays off. And you won't be if you become a Reconnaissance Man today.

Two, it only naturally follows that if you major in the wrong subject you will waste every second of your life futilely pursuing a career in its corresponding field. I wasted 18 years of my youth in banking. Another friend of mine wasted 25 in architecture. And the likes of Andrea Dworkin waste entire lifetimes in faux fields such as "women's studies." Life is just too short to wed yourself to careers you chose at the naïve age of 17. You can certainly limit your losses by cutting bait and trying a different degree or field, but it's infinitely more efficient to become a Reconnaissance Man first, figure out who you are, and then choose the right career the first time around.

Finally, Americans easily waste 30 years a piece living in places they really don't want to live. They're too busy trying to make ends meet, putting food on the table, and staying out of debt, that it isn't until their children leave the house do they finally ask themselves, *"Well, where do we **want** to live?"* Invariably, however, they all choose the same places. Specifically warm, low-tax places.

Arizona.
Florida.
Nevada.
The Carolina's.
Texas.
Tennessee.

Even South Dakota.

The question I often ask myself is why don't the youth of today look at what the older people are doing and say, *"Hey, you know, these old timers might know something I don't! Maybe I ought to follow their lead?"*

Why live 30 years in Cleveland dealing with snow, local income taxes, and decaying buildings when you know you're going to move to Florida anyway?

Why live in Milwaukee where you get the same, plus a chance of getting shot, when you know you really want to live in sunny Phoenix?

And why the hell would you stay in New York City, suffering the traffic, cost of living, and high unemployment, when you know moving to Dallas would make all those problems go away?

In taking the time to find out about yourself and become a Reconnaissance Man you will literally save yourself DECADES of life avoiding worthless degrees, careers that weren't for you, all while living in states that just suck. And since most people only have eight decades of life, not wasting those 20, 30, or even 40 years can dramatically improve your life.

"Finding Yourself"

When people say "finding yourself" they are usually referring to a 43 year old soccer mom who "just isn't haaaappyyyyy," up and divorces her husband, leaves her family, and travels to Europe to "find herself."

That is NOT what we're talking about when it comes to being a Reconnaissance Man.

What we are talking about is the important pursuit of self-knowledge and self-discovery. To know who you are, what you stand for, and what you want out of life. Logically, it makes the most sense to answer these questions early in life as possible (not when you're 43, married, with children, and already 50% dead) because if you can answer these questions early on, then the path for the remainder of your life is clear. Sadly, most people do not become Reconnaissance Men, pursuing self-knowledge and self-discovery early in life as possible. They opt instead to stumble through life, with no direction, point, or purpose and hope things magically go their way. Soon they *are* that 43 year old soccer mom, and in a desperate, panicked attempt to recoup what youth they've lost they have a mid-life crisis. They travel to Europe, they get a sports car, they get a divorce, date someone half their age, or they quit their career and join some hippy-dippy religion.

Reconnaissance Men never have to face that fear.

In taking the time to do reconnaissance, find out where you want to live, and all the self-discovery that comes with that journey, you will inevitably find out what it is you want out of life. This will not only provide a clear road map towards your life goals, but give you the confidence and peace of mind that comes with having such knowledge. You won't worry that you don't have a degree while your 22 year old peers do. You won't worry that you don't have a McMansion at 30 while the Jones next door do. And you'll never have that nagging doubt you're not pursuing your dreams and living the life you want. You will have determined your fate and path in life as you simply refused to "let life happen to you," and because of that you will have a life most others envy - a regretless one.

Happiness

The benefits of becoming a Reconnaissance Man are many and varied, but ultimately they all lead to the same thing – increased happiness.

In simply taking the time to explore this country, your place in it, and discovering yourself in the process, you will have such an advantage over your peers you will be light years ahead of them. Your finances will be better, your social life will be better, your love life will be better, your mental and physical health will be better, and you will have easily saved decades of life over your contemporaries. Nearly every aspect and facet of life will be better.

This isn't to say you're in a competition with your peers or that you would measure your success by others' failures. It is merely to point out that happiness is the definition of success in life and what everybody should aim for. But if we look at the vast majority of people, we realize they aren't happy, or at least aren't as happy as they could have been. And the reason why is they blindly did what others told them to without first taking the time to ask themselves what they wanted out of life. If you can avoid this cardinal mistake by becoming a

Reconnaissance Man, you will drastically increase your chances of being happy and that is all that really matters in life.

PART II
PRACTICUM

CHAPTER 3
LOGISTICS, FINANCE, AND EDUCATION

Exploring the entirety of the United States before you're 25, let alone 18 is a daunting, if not, an outright impossible task. If you hope to do a decent job of it, you must be incredibly efficient with your time, resources, and money and put a lot of forethought and planning into it. Key to all of this, however, will be to kill as many birds as possible with one stone, achieving multiple tasks at the same time. So while frugality, budgeting, and common sense will certainly go a long way, ensuring you don't waste a single second that could be spent double or triple dipping is how you will successfully pull off becoming a Reconnaissance Man.

The key challenges you'll face while conducting reconnaissance are:

- Logistics
- Finance, and
- Education

We will discuss how to meet these challenges in their own individual rights, but also highlight how they overlap so you can resolve two or three of them at the same time.

Logistics

Logistics entails the entire smorgasbord of planning, preparation, lodging, traveling, food, operations, and even hygiene that will be required to effectively and efficiently tour the entire country. Logistics is of primary importance because it determines everything else - the total cost of your endeavor, how much time you'll spend doing reconnaissance, how much of the country you'll see, how much you'll learn, not to mention whether you're doing it in comfort or misery. Therefore you must invest adequate time contemplating, considering, and planning the logistics of your reconnaissance. Or as I like to say, *"An hour at the drawing board, will save a day in the field"* because planning and preparation are the most important and economic part of logistics.

Planning & Preparation - Time

The single most limiting variable you are going to face becoming a Reconnaissance Man will not be money, but time. In the ideal world you will immediately start traveling the country upon getting your driver's license. This will give you, at most, two years of subsidized travel because you live at home with your parents. But once you turn 18 (or your parents cut the purse strings), you will not only have to support yourself, but also work up enough money to finance yourself in the field for weeks, even months at a time. And employers don't necessarily like employees who get up and leave for weeks or months at a time.

Because of this, the ideal situation is to start reconnaissance the first summer you get your driver's license. Admittedly, that is likely moot for the majority of readers, but still, in the ideal world the day you can legally drive is the day you start your journey to become a Reconnaissance Man. However, whether you're 16 or 26, there is a common variable in both instances – summer. And this variable, more or less, lays down the timeline by which most people will plot their reconnaissance.

First, whether you're in high school or college you get summers off. You don't have to attend school and for the most part nobody is seriously expecting you to work a real job, let alone for the entire summer. This allows you to build up the finances during the school year necessary to finance at least a two week expedition into the United States. You assume three summers where you are still living at home but can legally drive (sophomore/junior summer, junior/senior summer, and senior/college freshman summer) and that is six weeks of total exploration time. You assume 16 hours per day of potential driving time at 60 miles per hour, you can, in theory, cover over 40,000 miles. The entire US interstate highway system is only 48,000 and that includes the thousands of miles of vast, boring nothingness the plains states and the traffic-clogged east coast states have to offer. Of course, this assumes you're constantly pushing the pedal to the metal and taking no time to explore any cities, but it does show you it is mathematically possible to explore most of the country before you head off to college.

Second, it's not like once you leave home you can't afford to road trip for two weeks. Your average college student, 20 something, and (certainly) 30 something can carpool with a bunch of other aspiring Reconnaissance Men and easily afford two weeks in the field during summer. Assuming you do three summers of reconnaissance during high school and three more the following summers, you not only would have easily flown past the theoretical "Stage 1" of reconnaissance, but would be well on your way into "Stage 2," having two week stays in, at minimum, three to four towns.

Finally, summer allows for seasonal and migratory work. This allows you to stay in the field longer because you're replenishing your funds, though you may have to remain stationary to work for a couple weeks. Still, while the…

rafting guides I met in Glacier National Park, the Sturgis girl bartenders I met in South Dakota, and the staff who rented me my Jeep in Moab

all had to work, once they had a day off, they were out there exploring a different part of the country they had never seen before. And, once their two weeks or month was up, some (notably the Sturgis girls) would move on to the next tourist destination to work and explore there. Therefore, you don't have to make a rushed two week mad-dash across the country, but can take a more paced (though laborious) approach and find various places to work during summer, allowing you three entire months to explore this great country.

Now admittedly not everybody will be able to pursue this strategy. If you're out of school you likely don't have summers off. If you have a seasonal career you're typically working summers and not working winters. Or some of you have kids, which exponentially increases the cost and complexity of conducting reconnaissance. Still, there should be some way to go on a two week expedition every year into the US, which over three to four years, will allow you to find out where you want to live. The entire process may take five years, and you could very well be 40 by the time you finally figure out where you belong. But that's better than how most people do it, waiting until they're 65 and nearly dead to live where they really wanted to.

Planning & Preparation – Strategy

The bank I worked at in Wyoming was so atrociously inefficient and mal-managed that I rarely had a day where I worked more than two hours. So out of boredom I'd often find myself conducting unnecessary economic research, going for extended motorcycle rides to conduct "site visits," taking two hour lunches, and otherwise suffering the literal hell that is known as "looking busy." However, summer was coming up and I started to wonder what the quickest route to Alaska by motorcycle was. And so I spent an entire afternoon looking at potential routes.

At first Google plotted the most direct and efficient route to a town called Hyder, Alaska, but then I started to notice a couple things. One, the most direct route was not the most scenic as I would largely miss what the Canadian Rockies had to offer - Banff, Jasper, Revelstoke, and Lake Louise. Two, it said nothing about the final leg of the journey from Kitwanga to Stewart which was 136 miles, but had no gas stations. Meanwhile, my bike only had a range of 120 miles. Three, after doing some math, I realized the number of miles I'd be putting on my bike would require a couple oil changes and likely a new tire. This required incorporating the town of Prince George into my plans since it was the only town in the area that had the supplies and mechanics I would need. In the end, I ended up spending nearly three full days researching the trip and all of the logistics that would be involved.

And I'm glad I did.

Because not only did I get to see the most beautiful scenery I've ever seen in my life, but sure enough I did need oil changes, a jerry can of gas, a new tire,

AND a new fuel pump. It was only because I had the foresight to stop in Prince George and have my bike looked over was I not stranded in the hinterlands of Canada for a week with a hefty lodging and towing bill to boot.

Such foresight and planning is also required before you go out into the field.

To ensure you don't waste precious time in the field, it pays tremendous dividends to fully research where you want to go and more importantly where you DON'T want to go. In the olden days if you wanted to know if you'd genuinely like to visit a place you'd have to read a book about it, or more likely, actually go there. This was a considerable risk since you'd have to gamble significant time, money, and resources on the bet you would maybe, theoretically, possibly, like the place. But today with the advent of the internet you can research anything and in such great detail you can usually determine this without having to expend the time and resources to get there. This is a huge benefit because you can narrow your search with such precision you're unlikely to waste any time visiting a place you'd hate. The trick, however, is not waiting until two weeks before you head off into the field and then hastily research some destinations. You need to plan during the entire year in anticipation. And what better place to plan than at school or work?

To be honest, school and work are not only boring, they're highly inefficient. Nobody works a full eight hours a day because most managers and bosses are very mediocre people and lack the organizational skills to keep their employees' plates full. Teachers and professors are even worse where you don't even have to show up to class to pass it. Ergo, you can easily spend an hour per week at work or in class, pulling up maps, reading reviews, and conducting a preliminary digital reconnaissance to plan for the real thing. So by the time you're ready to go into the field you should already have a pretty good idea of

1. Where you want to go
2. What you want to see
3. What you want to do, and
4. What else is in the area

Having this well-thought out and planned itinerary will make it infinitely easier (and more affordable) to become a Reconnaissance Man.

Planning & Preparation – Mapping and Scheduling

Once you have your list of destinations you need to divvy them up into digestible chunks your summer excursions can handle. And if your entire destination list can be done in two weeks, you're doing it wrong and need to go back to the drawing board and come up with some more. You should have AT MINIMUM three trips worth (or six weeks' worth) of destinations to do a decent job of the US. But regardless of how many you choose and where they are, geographical proximity will likely be the determining variable of how you group your destinations and plan your visits. Here I strongly recommend you group them based on the weather because climate can easily determine whether you're outside enjoying life…or driving off an icy Colorado cliff…or being rushed off to an Arizona hospital for heat stroke.

For example, visiting the upper Rockies in Idaho, Montana, Colorado and Wyoming is all great fun…in July. If you go in March, or even September, not only will you have to deal with snow, but cold temperatures and brutal winds because you're usually above 7,000 feet.

Arizona is another great example. I love Arizona. It has the Grand Canyon, great motorcycle riding, picturesque towns like Sedona and Jerome, but it's insufferable in July. One week while visiting my buddy down there the temperature NEVER dropped below 100, with highs regularly above 110. You're immobile, you can't do anything. You just suffer going from one air-conditioned building to the next, with intermittent stops in an air-conditioned car. It makes reconnaissance impossible.

Therefore, I'd strongly recommend doing any southern destinations in early spring, late fall, perhaps even the dead of winter. Any mid-state or plain state destinations are OK during the summer. And do not visit Glacier National Park, Alaska, Idaho, or Colorado unless it's the Dog Days of summer.

In addition to timing your trips wisely, it also pays to travel them in the most efficient manner possible. This is actually quite easy today as Google maps will provide you the most efficient route to save you time, money, and gas. However, this assumes you stick to the plan. The size of the United States cannot be overstated and there are literally thousands of things to see. You'll constantly be tempted to divert from the plan, drive down this road or check this other thing out. But unless absolutely compelling (say, you didn't realize the Grand Canyon was in Arizona) you likely can't afford to deviate from the plan. This doesn't mean you're a robot strictly adhering to some computer protocol. You can certainly have some flexibility in your schedule and you should. But if this is the case or you are more of the roaming vagabond type, you will want to budget extra money, extra time, perhaps even an extra trip into your itinerary.

Choosing a Mode of Transportation

Choosing a mode of transportation that ideally fits your plans is very simple because I'm going to choose for you. You WILL drive a car. You WILL road trip. You will NOT fly, take a train, bus, or boat. And enticing as it may be, you will not drive a motorcycle. The reasons why are many and vital.

First, you need to be mobile and versatile. Since the purpose of reconnaissance is exploratory, you need a vehicle that allows you to do that. If you take a bus, a plane, or a train, you're restricted only to the areas they service and a lot of the country cannot be reached by plane, train, or bus.

Second, buses and trains are too slow. They make way too many stops and you simply don't have the time to be sitting at a bus stop in Hartford, Wisconsin or a train stop in Havre, Montana. Planes may be faster, but only if you're traveling to major cities. If you wish to get into the less-populated areas of the country, you'll need a "puddle jumper" flight which not only takes more time that you don't have, but also increases the cost of a flight exponentially.

Third, lodging. Though we'll discuss it in more detail, a car provides you a 24-7 form of emergency lodging should you need it. This not only allows you to theoretically cut your lodging budget to $0, but allows you to adapt to any unexpected problems that may (and will) pop up during your trip.

Fourth, you need to see the entire country, not fly over it just to see a patch of it elsewhere. Part of reconnaissance is to get to know the country extensively so you know what is out there, what you'd like to explore, and what else is surrounding your pre-selected destinations. Furthermore, the truth is every city in America is more or less the same with Wal-Marts, McDonald's, and strip malls in the burbs, and slowly rotting downtown cores with night clubs, office buildings, and boutique coffee shops that go in and out of business every week. So flying from one major city to the next is really no different than if you took a flight, circled around a bit, and merely landed back at your home town. You need to get out of the city and a car is the ideal mode of transportation to do that.

However, all these compelling reasons to use a car aside, there is one major reason that supersedes them all.

A car is how you will find yourself.

Reconnaissance is a journey that will help you find yourself. Understand that for all of your life you've been forced to go to a literal mental prison known as school. At school you are not intellectually challenged or stimulated. And though your teachers may have been trying to get you to think about the future, what you'd like to become, and somehow inspire you, most of them are so mediocre, boring, and incompetent they likely instead put you to sleep. Again, you'd like to think after 17 years of K-college schooling you'd have a very good idea of what you wanted to do in life, but the truth is just to get through that mind-numbing prison you turned off your brain and went into a semi-catatonic state, giving not one second of thought to your future.

Sadly, this means it's not until college is over do most people have the time, let alone the energy, to contemplate what they want to do in life. Worse, it's not like this is an easy decision as if you're choosing between chocolate and strawberry ice cream. It's a critical life choice you have to make that will take contemplation, introspection, thought, and above all else, time.

Which is precisely what a road trip across the country offers.

If you're on a plane, flying from one town to the next, you don't have the time to sit down and ponder the meaning and purpose of your life. You have to get through the TSA, put your shoes back on, rush to the gate, pay attention to what zone they're calling, get on the plane, and then rush to grab your things as you all disembark. But if you have to drive to Albuquerque from Akron, you got yourself an easy 1,500 miles of Indiana-Iowa-Kansas quiet nothingness to drive through. And I assure you the amount of time you'll spend thinking about your future during that one way trip will be infinitely more than all the time you thought about it during your 17 years of school.

In other words, road tripping is a VITAL part of reconnaissance and you cannot become a Reconnaissance man without it. You need to have all that time on the road alone to start thinking about where you belong, what you want to do, and what you want to become. Your thoughts cannot be interrupted by security checkpoints, an uncomfortable train, or a herpes-infected bum who talks your ear off on the bus. You need a car with a comfortable seat, a full tank of gas, the radio off, and preferably, solitude.

Vehicular Maintenance

Ideally, your journey to becoming a Reconnaissance Man would start at the age of 16. But since so few of us had this insight at such an early age, it's most likely you are a 20 or 30 something whose been wandering the desert trying to look for purpose and focus in life. In either instance, chances are you don't have a ton of money and therefore can't afford a reliable vehicle. Unfortunately, you NEED a reliable vehicle if you're going to traipse all over a 2,700 mile wide country, and it is here, depending on your age, you have two options.

One, you can rent a car. Truthfully, this is the ideal option. The car is unlikely to break down, most rental companies allow you unlimited mileage, and even if the car does break down, you don't have to pay for it. The problem is you have to be at least 21 to rent a car in most states, so you intrepid 16 year olds are going to be SOL on this one.

Your second option is to use your own car, which in all likelihood is not as reliable or in good of shape as a brand new rental. Chances are it will break down, requiring some kind of maintenance and repair. However, even here we have the opportunity to slay two birds with one stone in that we can learn to become mechanics.

While you may not be able to drive at the age of 13, nothing says your father can't teach you how to do basic and not so basic mechanical work on a car until the point in time you can drive. Again, putting the effort into pre-planning, you can become quite the accomplished auto-mechanic in three years if you start at the age of 13. Of course, not all fathers are mechanics themselves, not to mention most fathers today just aren't around. But you can replace your father with "Daddy YouTube" where there is nearly every tutorial imaginable for one to teach themselves auto-mechanics.

Regardless of how you learn auto-mechanics, it is theoretically possible for a 16 year old to have a set of tools, some spare parts, a used car, and the mechanical ability to keep it running perpetually in the field. This will not only provide for reliable (and cheap) transportation for conducting reconnaissance, but will give a young man or woman a skill infinitely more employable than a liberal arts degree – auto-mechanics.

Lodging - Camping

Lodging can easily be your biggest expense or your smallest. It all depends on how much you want to rough it versus how luxurious you demand your accommodations be. But since most of you are younger not only can you rough it, chances are you can't afford lodging anyway, making the issue of lodging moot. Thankfully, you don't need four star hotels to rest your precious little head, you just need a place that's cheap, safe, and clean. And here you have plenty of options.

If you're a fan of camping, a basic tent or "Hennessy Hammock" (a self-sealing hammock) will more than suffice. For added comfort you can bring an air mattress, but for anyone who enjoys hiking or the outdoors, camping will likely be your preferred option. However, the key issue with using a tent or hammock will be finding a convenient area to legally camp. For the most part you can't camp at waysides, requiring you to pay for a camp site either at a KOA or a state/national park. Thankfully, there are two ways you can camp for free.

One, while you have to pay to camp in a national PARK you do not have to pay to camp in a national FOREST or national GRASSLAND. Matter of fact (as of 2016) you're quite free to do whatever you want in national forests and grasslands as they are considered public lands – i.e. yours. You can camp for free, camp wherever you want, have a fire (assuming there is no fire ban), and shoot guns. Better yet, national forests and grasslands are all over the nation making it relatively easy to find a convenient camp site. Additionally, a lot of national forests are actually more beautiful than a lot of national parks, providing you infinitely better scenery than you'll ever find at a 5-star hotel.

Two, there are free places to camp across the United States. You just have to know where they are. Thankfully, the following site lists all of them and is a personal MUST-VISIT site for me:

https://freecampsites.net/

<u>Lodging - Car</u>

While not terribly comfortable, your car still makes for great lodging on the cheap. It's a solid structure, it has a heater if needed, and you can more or less park it anywhere (preferably near a public toilet) and sleep. It also has an additional advantage over camping – it's much faster. The problem with camping is you have to find a site, pitch a tent, lay down your bedding, and then undo it all the next morning. It's at minimum an hour-long process. A car you simply pull the seat lever, fall back, and go to sleep. The next morning, pull the seat lever, sit up, and drive. This proves particularly beneficial if you're tight for time.

But time-savings aside, the car does have a couple drawbacks. First you need to aerate the vehicle otherwise condensation will build in the car. This isn't a major issue, but it can get stuffy, even moldy if you don't let some air in. The solution may simply be to open a window, but then you get to deal with mosquitos that will ensure you never get a decent night's rest. You'll either need to vent your car or put in a screen window (which takes some jerry-rigging and lots of duct tape). Second, while you can stay at waysides with a car, in most states you are technically only allowed to stay a couple hours. The camp sites, national parks, state parks, and hotels don't want you sleeping at places for free and have lobbied most state governments to limit the time somebody can stay at a wayside. However, in my now-approaching 30 years of sleeping at waysides I have NEVER had a cop interrupt my slumber and tell me to move on.

Still, if you're harassed or the local constable orders you to move on, it's not that hard to find a free place to park your car and sleep. I've slept in neighborhoods, cul-de-sacs, church parking lots, gas stations, Wal-Marts, you name it. The key thing is to make sure a public and 24-7 toilet is nearby which makes Wal-Mart and gas stations ideal places to catch some z's.

Lodging - Van

Take everything that was said about cars and add the benefit of more comfortable bedding, with the drawback of poorer fuel efficiency. While not my preferred means of cheap lodging, this is largely due to the fact I'm a short small guy and can fit quite comfortably in the back seat of most cars. However, if you're a taller or larger individual you're going to have a hard time sleeping in a Kia Rio, and therefore may want to consider paying a little extra in gas to get the comfort that comes with a van.

Lodging - Facebook Friends

Whether you're in the field for two weeks or three months, chances are you're going to miss sleeping in a real bed. But while you may not have the budget to stay at a hotel, you likely have some friends you've met over the internet who happen to live in areas you intend to visit. This presents not only a great opportunity for some free lodging and a warm shower, but a chance to form valuable lifelong friendships that you never knew were possible.

Of course, your mother's mind will immediately default towards you being chopped up into itty bitty bits by a mass-murdering Jeffrey Dahmer, but the truth is you've likely established some very good, trustworthy friendships online over the years and know these people as if they lived next door. Some of the greatest friendships I've made have been over the internet, and of course, this has conveniently resulted in the fringe benefit of a lot of free lodging. But there's much more to meeting digital friends in meatspace than some free lodging and a warm shower, and this plays a vital role in your journey to become a Reconnaissance Man.

One, it's lonely out there. Spending two weeks (let alone an entire summer) driving across unfamiliar territory will take its inevitable psychological toll. You're all alone, in unfamiliar territory, and while you're really in no threat of danger, you'll still have this constant nagging fear in the back of your head that will wear on you. Invariably, humans are social animals and you will need human interaction, if for any other reason than to re-base yourself and your psychology. So to keep your spirits and morale up it pays to drop in on some friends and have some human interaction and conversation.

Two, laundry.

Laundry is its own logistical issue, but directly relates to hygiene. And whereas you can wear jeans for so long they develop sentience and start walking on their own, things like underwear and ESPECIALLY socks can result in athlete's foot or worse, trench foot. It's always good to stop in and visit a digital buddy just so you can wash your socks and underoos.

Three, new friendships.

The most important thing in life is other people. And some of the most important other people in your life will be your friends. But whereas in the olden days your choice in friends was relegated to your geographical area, the internet allows you to meet all 7 billion people in the world. This not only increases the number of friends you can have, but drastically increases your chances of making great life-long friends because of the filtering nature of social media. A mere 30 years ago you'd be lucky to meet a fellow "bartender, Jewish, fisherman" in your area as that unique combination of traits is relatively rare. But with the internet no doubt there is a 400 member group somewhere of "bartender Jewish fishermen.org," where people can meet to talk about being Jewish bartenders who have a passion for fishing. The point is the internet has made it so you can find "your people" and "your calling" infinitely easier than a generation ago. And when you meet these people, your shared interests, hobbies, philosophies, and intellects guarantee you'll make some great life-long friends.

This, I would argue, is a vital part of reconnaissance unto itself. Yes, you want to spend some time alone, traveling the country, figuring out your place in life. But it is imperative you also capitalize on the opportunity to meet your fellow internet brothers and sisters of the "Fraternal Order of Bartender Jewish Fishermen." Life is just too short not to.

<u>Lodging - CouchSurfing.com</u>

If you insist on having a couch and a shower, but don't have a network of internet friends a happy compromise might be to consider CouchSurfing.com. Couch Surfing is basically a website where different people across the world allow you to stay for free on their couch. While its lodging benefits are apparent, it's largely a social site for adventurers and explorers to meet like-minded people and in a karmic way "pay it forward" to fellow travelers.

However, while you may be tempted by the free lodging and warm showers, there is a key drawback to Couch Surfing. You don't know who you're staying with. Though rare, muggings, rape, and just uncomfortable situations can and do happen. This requires you couch surf with caution and common sense.

Naturally, you'll want to thoroughly vet everybody who is offering lodging. Read all of the reviews of previous travelers, google search the person to find out all you can, and meet that person first for coffee. You'll also want to tell people back home who you're staying with and where, as well as have a Plan B for housing in case your host proves untrustworthy. The best way to screen hosts, however, is like anything else with logistics – planning.

CouchSurfing.com has meetups in nearly every major and medium-sized town where you can go and meet fellow couch surfers. You may not need lodging in your hometown, but you can get involved in the community, meet people you trust, and usually they have recommendations of trustworthy hosts they can refer you to in towns you wish to visit. Again, this requires a little bit of upfront work before you go off into the field, but can pay off in terms of time, money, safety, and future friendships.

Lodging - Air BNB

If camping, sleeping at waysides, or crashing on strangers' couches still doesn't cut it, then chances are you'll need to get a hotel. This will drastically increase your costs, making reconnaissance too expensive for most people, but you can seriously mitigate these costs by using Air BNB.

Based on the website http://priceonomics.com/hotels/ Air BNB rooms are about 50% cheaper than your average hotel room in the US. Even full apartments are 20% cheaper than a mere hotel room. Additionally, you can usually find longer term lodging accommodations through Air BNB than you will at a hotel. This will not only allow you to become a Reconnaissance Man in style, but can change your overall reconnaissance strategy. Instead of a mad dash across the US, sleeping at random waysides, you can headquarter at strategic places for a month at a time, allowing you to thoroughly road trip and explore that part of the country.

Still, taking this luxurious option will take a little bit of the rustic spirit out of becoming a Reconnaissance Man. You don't want this journey to be a pampered and spoiled one. You want it to be a challenge that forms you and molds you. So occasionally splurge on an Air BNB if you're in desperate need of a warm shower or a good night's sleep, but don't use it as a crutch and ruin the experience.

<u>Hygiene</u>

Closely related to lodging is hygiene as your choice in lodging will most certainly affect your hygiene. If you're lucky and your parents not only endorse your reconnaissance, but finance it too, you'll have comfy hotel rooms every night, replete with showers, soap, and shampoo. If you're not, chances are you'll be doing what I do – sleeping at waysides, washing in sinks. But like most other logistical issues, maintaining your hygiene will be a mere inconvenience and one you can easily overcome.

The first thing to realize is you don't need a shower or bathtub to fully and effectively wash your body. One merely needs fresh water, a bar of soap, some shampoo, and a wash cloth. This means any wayside with running water or a western mountain stream will do. Of course, picturesque as a western mountain stream may be, keep in mind it's basically water that was snow no more than 10 minutes ago and is usually frigid. Still, clean is clean, and be it a wayside sink or a 32.1 degree stream, it's a small price to pay for keeping your body clean.

Second, like your body, your clothes also need to be washed regularly. Here you have many options, some convenient, some not so much. Ideally, you'd have regularly-scheduled Facebook friends' places you'd be stopping in at to regularly wash your clothes. Next best would be to have a couple rolls of quarters to use at the inevitable laundromats you'll come across during your travels. However, if you find yourself in BFE, North Dakota chances are you won't have either of these luxuries. We once again visit our buddies the sink and the fresh water stream.

During college I lived on the 34th floor of a questionably safe building. It had a laundromat, but not only was it on the first floor, there was also a 50/50 chance somebody would steal your clothes if you didn't stay there to watch your laundry. So for the 18 months I lived there, my roommate and I would wash our clothes in the sink of our apartment and strategically hang our clothes about the apartment to dry.

This strategy led to a new discovery. While it was easy to wash socks and underwear, larger items like jeans, pants, and sweat shirts took much longer. Thankfully, those items were not as vital to wash as socks and underwear, so we would only wash those once a week. This epiphany has ramifications for reconnaissance as your sole focus for laundry should be on underwear and socks.

When you pack, the majority of your clothing should be underwear and socks.

When you have some free time at a way side, grab some shampoo and wash your underwear and socks.

While you're driving, dry your underwear and socks on the front or rear dashboard of the car.

And when your mom asks you what you want for Christmas? Underwear and socks.

I've gone two weeks in the field not washing my ratty old jeans and standard black hoodie with no major life complications. But there isn't a wayside in the

US where my underwear and socks haven't been washed. I suggest you do the same.

Finally, if you work out regularly and can afford it, it's a good idea to get a gym membership at a national chain like Anytime Fitness or Planet Fitness. These chains not only have gyms in every major and minor city, they also have showers that members can use for free. This kills two birds with one stone because you can shower and get some exercise as well. This will not only keep you clean and in shape, but the exercise will keep your morale up as well.

Food

While vital, food is one of the simpler logistical issues to solve. Prior to Wal-Marts or grocery stores being everywhere, one would have to pack a ton of non-perishable food in their car and slowly eat through this inventory as their trip progressed. This resulted in an incredibly boring diet of granola bars, beef jerky, apples, and soda. But while you might save yourself a couple bucks pilfering your parents' pantry, it's just easier and more convenient to stop in at your local grocery store or Wal-Mart and get some fresh fruit, veggies, and other non-perishable food items. Not only will the food be fresher, but you'll need to stretch your legs, walk around, clear your mind, and maybe even splurge on a $5 footlong.

Safety

While it's best to travel with others, chances are you're going to become a Reconnaissance Man on your own. Most people just can't take off three months or afford a summer long road trip across the country, and truthfully, most are too scared to. So to ensure you come back home and aren't buried in a shallow grave in the woods you'll need to take some safety precautions.

First, you'll want to check in daily with family or friends. Post to your Facebook account, text pictures, or just call to inform people where you are, who you're with, and where you are going. Second, as mentioned before, thoroughly screen the people you'll be meeting on your trip. Meet them in public places first with other people around. Don't commit to staying with people you haven't thoroughly vetted. Third, ensure your communication lines stay open. You don't want to be hiking in the middle of the Grand Escalante, get attacked by a mountain lion, and have your cell phone die. Keep your cell phone charged and even carry a spare burn phone.

Finally, carry a weapon. Your political passions about guns and pacifism are very cute. Now set those aside, become an adult, and man up. You are going out into the real world, by yourself, and there are evil people and things that will hurt you if given the chance. Robbers, rapists, thieves, drunks, and meth heads, and this says nothing about the number of animals in the wilderness that would like you for a snack. Ideally you would carry a .40 caliber or higher pistol with you (as 9MM is not large enough to take down most predatory animals), but depending on your age and the state you're in, you may not be allowed to legally carry a gun. If this is the case, bring mace (bear mace if going into the woods), an asp, a Quorum personal attack alarm, and train with them as well so you can effectively use them in case of an emergency.

How the Author Does Logistics

While everybody is different, to provide a working example I'll highlight how I personally conduct reconnaissance. This will hopefully give you a working model to start with, which you can then tailor to your specific needs and preferences.

Planning – I easily spend a week's worth of labor studying, researching, and investigating where I want to go and how I'm going to get there. A lot of this is due to the fact that I go to very remote places (Hyder, Alaska, Radisson, Quebec, etc.) and often take my motorcycle. This means gas becomes a huge issue, often requiring that I take a jerry can, as well as timing things like weather. In general, however, I usually pick a place that interests me, research it thoroughly, see what else is in the area, and then I plot a tentative route there and a different route back so as to maximize the new area I cover.

Vehicle – My main vehicle is a small, fuel-efficient Japanese import. I can comfortably sleep in the driver's seat. I have taught myself some basic mechanics through YouTube and am able to repair most non-major problems. I always bring my tool box as well as a can of fix-a-flat, spare spark plugs, oil, a one gallon jerry can, and duct tape.

Lodging – I always assume I'm going to be sleeping at a wayside or a Wal-Mart. This is in part because I don't have a strict itinerary and usually like to roam around a bit, so it provides me the versatility of sleeping anywhere, anytime. I refuse to camp because it takes too long, it's not as comfy as my car, and there's no guarantee of running water or toilets. Thankfully, however, I have a very large network of internet friends and am usually enroute to visit them. I crash at their places the vast majority of time. The only time I stay at hotels is if I'm on my motorcycle and my lodging plans fall through.

Hygiene – In being fortunate enough to have a large network of internet friends I'm usually showering and doing laundry at their places. However, 15 years ago the wayside sinks were my best friends. I'd wash and shampoo out of wayside sinks as well as do laundry. My laundry was minimal with some hiking shorts, running shoes, a couple undershirts, but most importantly five pairs of underwear and socks each. You can dry laundry very effectively on the hot hood of a car during summer or by splaying them over the back seat of your car while driving with the windows down.

Food – I usually do not pack food or water unless I intend on hiking or going to particularly remote parts of the continent (Alaska, British Columbia, etc.). The convenience of buying water and snacks at gas stations IMMEDIATELY off the highway allows me to cover a lot more ground than driving into town to find a grocery store. The main staple of my diet, however, is healthy fast food such as Subway or Chipotle.

Safety – I carry a .40 Glock when hiking and a 9MM Springfield XD9 when in town. I also enjoy shooting guns, so I often have an AR15 along with me in case I run into some open federal land. I have never had any trouble with bears or mountain lions, but have had plenty of trouble with meth heads and drunks, specifically in Wyoming. Drunk/high hicks are by far the biggest threat you'll run into out west so ensure you keep to yourself, or if you're a young lady, avoid closing time at rural bars.

Finance

The total cost of financing your reconnaissance will largely depend on you and your preferences. If you want to do the minimalist approach, wherein you're in the field for two weeks every year, living out of your car, and eating nothing but Sam's Club food, you can do that for about $600. If you want to go away for an entire summer, driving half of the US interstate system, while also staying at hotels every night and eating out for every meal, it will cost around $10,000. The choice is up to you and your wallet. But since most of you are likely younger, and therefore, poorer, the issue of finance will likely be the largest hurdle you'll face when becoming a Reconnaissance Man.

Thankfully, if you do it right, nearly anybody can afford the annual two weeks a year in the field. But there are two key expenses one must budget for. One that is easily affordable and another that presents a problem for the particularly younger Reconnaissance Men:

Operational expenses and a car.

"No Man With a Good Car Needs to Be Justified"

Operational expenses, in all honesty, present no real challenge to becoming a Reconnaissance Man. Assuming you drive 5,000 miles each trip you can expect to spend around $450 on gas. If you eat at a grocery store, $150 is more than enough to feed your gullet for two weeks. Even a 15 year old can work up that money while living at home rent free. The real issue is the car as it not only costs a lot of money to buy one, but people 21 and under (in some states, 25) can't legally rent one. So, unless your parents are going to be extra charitable and let you drive their car, most 20 year olds and younger are going to have to buy their own car.

This expense can easily torpedo any 16 year old's dream about becoming a Reconnaissance Man before he/she's 21. It also seriously delays your advancement in life as it prohibits you from conducting reconnaissance when it's most optimal to do so – while you're young. So the only real option you have is to buy one. This may prove to be a major obstacle to your average 17 year old, but...

suck it up buttercup.

Life is not easy, nor fair, nor just, nor kind. And whining about things has never gotten anybody anywhere. So unless you can convince your parents about the merits of reconnaissance and get them to lend you their car, your only option is to buy one. Thankfully, you have an advantage most 25 year olds don't.

Time.

Starting at the age you are legally allowed to work, you will want to not only start working up the money to buy a car when you're 16, you will also teach yourself the basics of auto-repair and auto-mechanics. Ideally, your father would be around to teach you this, but given the prevalence of divorce, single motherhood, and broken families, YouTube is likely going to be your best auto-mechanics teacher. Your goal in this endeavor will be to find a cheap car you can afford, that is reliable enough to last you in the field while conducting reconnaissance, while also developing the mechanical skills to ensure it doesn't break down at all.

This, obviously, will require you take a job, perhaps a second job, buy some tools, and exercise the discipline needed to self-teach yourself a field as challenging as auto-mechanics. And it will also take sacrifice as you'd certainly much prefer to play video games, hang out with friends, date, and party in college. Still, remember reconnaissance is not a short term experience you are hoping to enjoy in the here and now. It is a long term and vital investment you are making in yourself so that you have an infinitely better and happier future. This doesn't mean you don't go party, have fun, or chase girls/boys. But unlike every other average person, you are not average. You demand to have a better life overall. You need to plot and plan to become a Reconnaissance Man. And that requires reliable transportation, which you'll ensure by becoming a competent mechanic.

Working in the Field

The last job I had that actually required me to physically be there was in 1997. Yes, I worked many jobs in banking and finance since then, but in those now-approaching 20 years not ONE job during that time really required me to go to the office and physically be there. And the reason why is the internet.

The internet is an obvious game changer on many levels. Most business is conducted online. Most payments are automated, no longer requiring checks or a physical presence. And entire industries like publishers and record labels have been wiped out, replacing the old, corrupt, nepotistic, cronyistic system with the meritocratic internet. But businesses, employers, and (specifically) baby boomer bosses remain recalcitrant in one particular regard:

They insist you unnecessarily suffer a commute and physically show up to an office every day.

Thankfully, this is changing. In part due to Gen Xer's acceptance of technology and telecommuting, but also because of the entrepreneurial nature of younger people. The internet has made it very easy to make money online be it via computer programming, podcasting, self-publishing books, opening online stores, or any other sort of entrepreneurship. And frankly, most young people's lives are online. They are not only accustomed to it, but it's part of their being. So while the old guard of baby boomer bosses may not like it, Gen X and Millennials are more or less going to insist they work from the internet and not a cube.

This gives any aspiring Reconnaissance Man an additional option and with it, flexibility. Specifically…who says you have to go back home to work?

If you are particularly entrepreneurial and you dedicate the time to develop the skills, a young man or woman can find employment online which allows them, in theory, to perpetually be in the field. Since all you need is a laptop and an internet connection, this untethers you from a cubicle, office, or work station. And if you have a shoe string budget for your reconnaissance, a mere modicum of online income can sustain you indefinitely.

This, of course, would be ideal because you could bang out your entire reconnaissance in one shot. You'd just gallivant around the US, even the world, trying to find out where you belong, while collecting a paycheck the entire time. It would even make reconnaissance moot because if you have a location-independent job, then why would you settle on staying in one place? Regardless, such a fortunate form of employment would take a fair amount of preplanning, trial and error, work and effort, not to mention luck. You'd have to start young and expect to fail many times over before you'd find this unicorn of a job. Still, if you can pull it off, being able to work from a laptop is not only the ideal way to finance your reconnaissance, but the American Dream as well.

Education

In the spirit of killing as many birds with one single stone as possible, education also plays a major role in becoming a Reconnaissance Man. For not only are you in the field to find out where you want to live, you're also out there to inevitably find out who you are and what you want to do in life. This path invariably leads to education.

Unless you're one of the very few and very lucky people who knows precisely what they want to do in life, chances are you're like everybody else. Directionless, indifferent, and apathetic about your career. You may have attended college for what you thought you'd like to study, but in the end we all work soul-sucking jobs we must endure simply to pay the bills and put food on the table. Most of this comes from the aforementioned problems of forcing 17 year old children to choose what their life-long careers will be. It also comes from the school system sapping us of all our mental energies to the point we couldn't ponder what we really wanted out of life. But regardless of the reasons, we never took the time to sit down, focus, and answer these important questions for ourselves. Thus, like most other people, we've all made poor decisions about our educations and careers.

But now you have the time.

When you go out into the field you will have a ton of time to yourself. You will be in the car, all alone, cumulatively for weeks. You will be in your hotel or tent for days. And if you're smart you'll avail yourself of the hiking opportunities out west, giving you even more time to yourself. All of this time can be wasted on your mind wandering aimlessly or ***invested, purposefully focused on figuring out what you want to do in life.*** And it is here you will spend any mental down time you have not on pointless daydreaming, but on educating yourself in preparation for your future life and career.

The Four Types of Reconnaissance Education

There are four types of education you will be giving yourself while you are in the field:

A Philosophical Education,
A Pre-requisite Education,
An Employment Education, and
An Education in Entrepreneurship

A **philosophical education** is one to ultimately guide your life decisions and create a set of principles by which you want to live your life by. Are you a parasite? Are you a Machiavellian opportunist? Do you have no problems living off of others via welfare and food stamps? Or are you a truly independent and productive person? One who lives off of no one else? An appreciator of your fellow man? And somebody who wishes to achieve greatness in their life?

What about children? Do you want a family? Do you want to get married? And what will you do to ensure the future is better than the one you grew up in? What will you do to give your children the opportunities you may not have had? Or will you opt not to breed, fearing the world has seen its heydays and is now staged for a long term, painful decline?

How about religion? Do you believe in a god? Or are you an atheist? What about agnosticism? What compelling arguments are there from all three camps? And if you do believe in a god, which religion do you choose? Are you a Christian? Do you believe in Judaism? What about Hinduism or Buddhism? Do you even know what those are? And which, if any, correspond the best to your own personal beliefs and observations in life?

We could go on, but getting a good philosophical education is vital as it more or less forms and molds you as a person, creating the foundation for your personal beliefs, morals, and principles. This in turn not only governs how you will interact with other people and live your life, but ultimately determine if you are a good person, a successful person, and a happy person.

Unfortunately, one never really finishes their education in philosophy. It is a life-long education from which you never graduate. Fortunately, however, it is a 100% free education wherein you needn't blow $75,000 on some worthless liberal arts degree, but merely need to go to your local library and read some books. Better yet, podcasts and audio books make educating yourself in philosophy very conducive to becoming a Reconnaissance Man as you can listen to them while you're driving or hiking. Ergo, before I go out into the field, I easily download 40 hours of podcasts, audio books, sermons, lectures, and talk shows, and I strongly recommend you do the same.

Finally, while there is no right or wrong way to start educating yourself about philosophy, I recommend organizing your education a little bit by first focusing on the following sub categories with the following recommendations:

General Philosophy
- Stefan Molyneux (www.freedomainradio.com)
- "Meditations" by Marcus Aurelius http://ocw.mit.edu/courses/#linguistics-and-philosophy
- http://www.greatconversation.com/10-year-reading-plan
- https://archive.org/details/westernphilosoph035502mbp

Ethics and Morality
- https://www.youtube.com/watch?v=fHIWwUU3sgI
- https://www.youtube.com/watch?v=9EF4I7HM0zI
- http://www.goodreads.com/book/show/949401.The_Ethics_Toolkit

The Meaning of Life
- Viktor Frankl, "Man's Search for Meaning"
- https://www.youtube.com/user/phuckmediocrity

Logic
- The Socratic Method
- The Scientific Method

- https://www.youtube.com/watch?v=yu7n0Xzqtfa

Economics
- Ludwig Von Mises, "Human Action"
- https://www.youtube.com/watch?v=ejJRhn53X2M
- Adam Smith, "The Wealth of Nations"
- Ayn Rand, "Atlas Shrugged"

Religion
- "Major Religions of the World" by Marcus Bach
- "The World's Religions" by Ninian Smart

These issues may not be pressing now as you're barely able to scratch up enough money for gas, food, and rent. But they will become vitally important later in life when your mind turns from mere matters of survival to those of existence, morality, principles, and the afterlife.

The second type of education you'll be getting in the field is a "**pre-requisite education**." Like it or not, today's modern labor market requires you have some form of post-high school education. And since K-12 does such a poor job of preparing you for the basics, you basically have to re-take those same classes all over again.

Freshman comp.
English lit.
Women's Studies.
Diversity Uber Alles.
And a whole host of other liberal arts classes.

But let us be very clear why you're being forced to take essentially two years of pre-req classes that have nothing to do with your major. It helps employ the least employable people in the world – liberal arts graduates. Without mandating every year that millions of college students take classes they don't need, these veritably unemployable and talentless people would either be slinging coffee, stuck in the unemployment line, or living back at home with mommy and daddy. So political forces within the government and education system mandate you waste your time and money taking these unnecessary classes.

Fortunately, there are two ways around this – online classes and CLEP/DSST exams.

With the advent of the internet, **ACCREDITED** colleges are increasingly doing one of two things. They are either offering online classes themselves OR granting college credit if you take an online course through a third party "MOOC" (Massive Open Online Class) such as Coursera, Khan's Academy, Udacity, EdX, etc. This not only makes it possible for you to study and earn college credit while you're in the field, it is also much cheaper (and in the case of some MOOC's, free!). Of course, not all colleges are doing this and you'll want to ensure that you will indeed get credit if you take and pass a MOOC, but this allows you to bang out your pre-requisites, and affordably so while out in the field.

The second option is the College Level Examination Program ("CLEP") and DANTES Subject Standardized Tests ("DSST"). These programs essentially allow you to take a $20-$200 test to see if you have the required knowledge to pass a college course. If you pass the test, you are granted the corresponding college credit, allowing you to bypass the unnecessary time and expense of taking a worthless pre-requisite class. This not only makes CLEP's and DSST's an effectively free alternative to a college education, but like online classes, it allows you to study from anywhere, making them very conducive to becoming a Reconnaissance Man.

The only caveat with both CLEP's and DSST's is that most colleges will limit the amount of college credit you can earn from CLEP's and DSST's. In theory you could get an entire college degree with CLEP's and DSST's, but colleges and professors put money above your education. Therefore, some colleges will limit the number of credits they'll grant to CLEP/DSST classes, some will allow you to bypass the college courses they represent (but then require you take completely new courses anyway), and some will simply deny you any college credit by taking them. You need to research your college IN DETAIL and ensure they take as many CLEP/DSST credits as possible and if not, find yourself another school. In short, you should be able to eliminate at least a year's worth of pre-requisite classes through CLEP/DSST exams, ideally your first two years of college classes.

The third type of education you'll give yourself in the field is an "**employment education**." Specifically, an education that will give you the skills and qualifications you need to land a job and start a career. This, of course, presumes you already determined what your life career will be, ergo, it's unlikely many 17 year old Reconnaissance Men will be focusing on employment education. But if you are a college graduate, have done your wandering in the desert, or just happened to have your pre-reqs out of the way, you likely know precisely what you want to pursue as a career, and can therefore take the corresponding classes online while you're in the field.

Here we run into a problem, however, as very few colleges offer full **AND ACCREDITED** bachelor's degrees online. And those that do are still charging a pretty penny. Thankfully, there are currently two colleges that at least offer somewhat affordable accredited online bachelor's degrees, and they are Arizona State University and Western Governors University.

The only good degrees Western Governors University offers are in the field of IT and Accounting, as they lack traditional degrees in STEM such as chemical engineering, electrical engineering, etc. Thankfully, ASU offers a wide array of IT and STEM degrees that should land you a job outside the food service industry. This doesn't mean you're going to be relegated to these two online colleges and just the degrees they offer. The trend in education is for more and more colleges to offer accredited bachelors and master's degrees online, so it is very likely you'll see additional colleges offering accredited degrees in the near future. But if you need something now to finish your degree while also becoming a Reconnaissance Man these two colleges are good starting points.

Finally, you don't need to go to college to get an employable education. As the economy evolves, different and increasingly specialized skills are in demand that, frankly, no college offers degrees in. This is perfectly exemplified in the IT world where technology is changing so rapidly they demand certifications in specific programming languages, security protocols, etc., and couldn't care less what lethargic and outdated college degree you have. This not only makes getting an education in IT conducive to becoming a Reconnaissance Man, but could also make for the ideal Reconnaissance Man ***career***.

Right now I'm on a boat in Florida writing this because my career (being an author) doesn't require me to be anywhere at any time. My buddy Chad, who I just got off the phone with, informed me he was up till 1AM eating last night, didn't get up until noon, is about to go for a run, and will get to his work when he feels like it because he's a self-employed CPA. And my other buddy, Linda, travels the world with her laptop as she's the indispensable IT gal for a rather large company and negotiated she never has to go into the office as it's completely unnecessary. The advent of the internet has not only freed us from the classroom, but has also freed us from commutes, traffic jams, parking fees, and cubicles, allowing us to work from wherever we want. But all of that depends on if you choose the right career. Because if you do, you not only could feasibly finance your entire journey to become a Reconnaissance Man, you could be in the field indefinitely. It could be your career. Travelling from one place to another, visiting towns you've never been, making new and interesting friends along the way, with absolutely no schedule to adhere to at all - all of it is possible if you choose a profession that can be done from a laptop with internet access. It is a level of freedom previously available to only the richest of people, made accessible to us modern-day commoners via the internet.

The final education you'll receive in the field is one of **entrepreneurship.** And it's not so much an education, as much as it is a great opportunity for you to come up with successful and profitable business ideas.

I do not leave my house without a notepad. And the reason why is that nearly all my successful business ideas have come from either being on the road or on mountain trails. I'd be out in the middle of Nowhere, Oklahoma at 2AM or half way up Deseret Peak in Utah, and boom, out of nowhere I would get a good business idea. The reason why these great business ideas strike at 2AM in the middle of nowhere, or on remote mountainsides in Utah is because for the first time ever you've given your brain adequate time and solitude to successfully brainstorm. And if you don't have that notepad ready to write down your brilliant business idea at that moment you WILL forget it.

Regardless, what makes entrepreneurship arguably the most important education you'll receive in the field is because it can be the difference between slaving away in a cube for $40,000 a year and sitting on a Floridian beach drinking a mojito as you collect royalties of $400,000 a year. So take as many CLEP exams or DSST tests as you want, no college degree replaces a good idea. This doesn't mean you're guaranteed to come up with the next Microsoft or Facebook, but it is to say to be ready for it. Because the chances of you coming up with a successful business idea is infinitely higher road-tripping across America than it is sitting in a business meeting or getting your MBA.

CHAPTER 4
PSYCHOLOGICAL HURDLES

Your journey to become a Reconnaissance Man can be an enjoyable one...or not. And a lot of that depends on how much you prepare yourself psychologically for this endeavor. For while gallivanting around the country, skipping college, all for a cumulative two year road trip of self-discovery sounds great, you are going to be putting your body and mind through its paces. You will be gone for weeks, potentially years at a time, in lands that are foreign to you, never sleeping in your same bed, nor with the psychological comforts of home. Therefore, if you're not prepared, both in mind and body, becoming a Reconnaissance Man can become a chore, or even worse, a miserable experience you'll regret.

Loneliness

Unless you're bringing a buddy or meeting a lot of people along the way, chances are you will be alone for the majority of the time. This can be particularly intimidating if you're 16 or this is the first time you've really left home. Not only is there nobody to talk to, but from a Darwinistic sense of survival humans needed others to survive. Be it fighting off saber-tooth tigers or the warring tribe next door, the human brain has been conditioned for the past 2 million years to rely upon the presence and company of others for its survival. And without other people around, especially for extended periods of time, it will wear on your psyche.

There technically is no solution for this. It's genetic, it's instinctual, and as it just so happens, it's a good thing because being alone and enduring it will make you a stronger person in the long run. But you can ameliorate the loneliness and psychological wear by not only visiting friends, but through the liberal use of technologies that did not exist a mere 20 years ago.

For example, many of you are completely unaware of the concept of "long distance phone calls." Until cell phones were invented it could be costly to merely call your parents since they were out of state. This cost resulted in me not calling my parents, or anybody back home, during college for a full three months. However, today you have cell phones and can pretty much call anyone, anywhere, anytime unless in a particularly remote part of the country.

Avail yourself of this technology by calling your mother, calling your dad, and calling your friends while you're adventuring about.

Akin to cell phones is social media. Facebook, Myspace, Twitter, texting, sexting, attaching photos. Practically all of human interaction has been digitized and is able to be conducted over the internet and smart phones. Share your experiences, interact with people online, and even though it's illegal and you "should never do it," texting or Facebooking over the internet I've heard makes trips across Nowheresville, Kansas much more tolerable.

Finally, remember your secondary objective of educating yourself in the field. You should have ample podcasts, audio books, lectures, etc., on your smartphone that should more than keep your mind off the fact you're alone. Matter of fact, if you do it right you'll end up being like me where you'll be so engrossed in a podcast or lecture, that you'll actually get upset when somebody calls you, immediately sending their interrupting phone call into voicemail.

Still, if this is your first time away from home or you just happen to know you are a very sociable person, it might pay to incorporate as many visits to internet friends or extended family members as possible into your reconnaissance plans. It's practically guaranteed that if you're lonely, sad, or depressed from a lack of interaction, your mind will not be focused on exploring the country or self-discovery. It will be homesick, daydreaming about your return home, and not the world in front of you. Ensure you have the human interaction necessary to keep your spirits up and make you want to stay in the field.

Intimidation

When first driving out West there was something bothering me in the back of my mind. It wasn't the vastness or nothingness of the West. Nor was it the lack of people and civilization. Not even the meth heads or drunks itching for a fight were concerning me.

It was the lack of water.

It took me a while to figure it out, but after pondering it for some time I realized that the absolute lack of water was taking a small, but real psychological toll on me. What if I was stranded? How would I survive out here? How do these people survive out here? What if it doesn't rain? What if the dam broke? Will we all die of thirst?

It wasn't until later did I learn about water tables, aquifers, wells, and reservoirs did I realize there was never any real threat of dying from thirst. But by simply being in an environment different from the one I grew up in, there was an element of intimidation I endured just like the claustrophobia my Wyoming colleague had whilst in Minnesota, and the apprehensiveness about vast jungles my girlfriend had in Mexico.

All of this is completely normal and it is a guarantee you too will endure this intimidation.

Again, like loneliness, being intimidated by a different environment is based in genetics and Darwinistic survival instincts. Your brain doesn't want to die, and when it comes across an environment it's not accustomed to, it will send you constant signals that something is wrong or about to go wrong. Most of this will come from the vast nothingness of the West, and will increase in intensity the further away you get from home. But it can also be amplified by drastically different environments.

If you're a country boy, you are likely intimidated by the traffic of Chicago.

If you're a city girl, you're likely intimidated by the lack of roads, gas stations, and infrastructure in North Dakota.

If you're a southern gentleman, you're intimidated by driving in the snow-packed Canadian mountains. And if you're from the north, you'd be uncomfortable driving across the Arizona desert in July with a quarter tank of gas.

Thankfully, unless you run into particularly remote parts of Nevada, Texas, Wyoming, Alaska, or northern Canada, the United States and Canada are not only amply populated, but are very safe. There is adequate infrastructure, population, gas stations, cell phone towers, cops, etc., that unless attacked by a bear in Montana or immediately killed in a car crash in Chicago, you will survive your reconnaissance. You will not be stranded, you won't get lost, you won't die of thirst, and you will not be eaten at Donner Pass.

Social Ostracization

Keep in mind most people do not become Reconnaissance Men. The vast majority of people don't take the time to think, inventory, contemplate, organize, and appreciate their finite lives, and therefore fail to embark on a journey that ensures they make the most of it. Most are mindless sheeple who do what they're told, obediently complying with what society tells them, who end up living quite unremarkable and pointless lives in the end. And since you're not going to conform with the herd and since you're going to demand more from life, there's going to be some psychological prices to pay. Namely, social ostracization.

Like loneliness and intimidation, the causes for social ostracization also have their origins in genetics. Specifically, tribalism. Once again, for most of human history we survived through numbers or belonging to "tribes." This means people have a genetic preference for their team, even though it may not be logical or based in reality, because whether you lived or died trumped whether your tribe was right or not.

Having racial preferences.

Having religious preferences.
Even getting emotionally invested in a sports team to the point you attack a fan of another team is an example of irrational tribalism.

So when you decide that you're going to be different and "leave the tribe," people get upset, they get angry, and some even seek their pound of flesh because in their unconscious, caveman instinctual brain you're leaving the tribe. And in doing so not only are you lessening their chances of survival, but implicitly making the statement you're better than them. This results in a whole host of psychological and social costs you will bear.

First, you will likely be socially ostracized either purposely or by the fact you're going into the field. Some people will be envious you are taking a different path than them. Some will be disparaging, mocking you for not attending college or for going on some "hippie trip." And others may have no genuine ill will towards you, but by the mere fact you're taking the path less travelled, you will be physically self-ostracized from the rest of your peers. You won't be at college. You won't be at parties. You won't be at the night clubs. You'll be at the Kearny, Nebraska wayside washing your socks in the sink.

Second, while the "herd's" genetics are instinctually against you, so are yours. Your genes have survived these past 2 million years by going with the tribe. Obedience and conformance is hard-wired into your brain. So skipping college, leaving your friends and family behind, and taking the unknown path in life will cast at least a modicum of doubt in your own mind. This will at times make you question yourself and shake your confidence, but these are the mental costs that come with blazing your own trail.

And then there's just petty and mean people. I can't count the number of clients whose family and friends mocked them, ridiculed them, even disowned them if they didn't conform, obey, and do precisely what they wanted them to. They didn't view their friend or child as a sovereign, independent person with their own dreams and wants. They viewed them as property of either the family or the tribe. And if that property dared to leave the community, the religion, even the family business, they were accused of many horrific and horrible things.

"Acting white." "An apostate." "A traitor."

These despicable people sadly love themselves and the tribe more than they do the individual who is presumably their friend or even their own child. And they are tyrants who obviously have no respect for an individual's right to their own future. If it's not already hard enough to become a Reconnaissance Man, imagine what it's like without the support of your family and friends.

Not Keeping Up With the Joneses

One of the more curious and common clients I have are those who chose not to go to college and instead worked during their late teens and early 20's. They stereotypically have some kind of a job, if not the beginnings of a proto-career such as a nursing assistant, entry level mechanic, or even the military. They also typically live at home and therefore not only have no debts, but also have savings of anywhere from $5,000 to even $40,000. But sure enough, right at the age of 22 they contact me at Asshole Consulting because they have a problem. And that problem is...all their high school friends are now graduating from college and they feel that they're behind or are somehow losers in life. All I can do is laugh.

For while your average corporal in the US Army feels inferior to his college graduating peers,

or

your average bartender feels ashamed she didn't graduate from college with her twin sister,

or

your typical self-taught auto-mechanic doesn't view his 2-year vocational degree as on par with a "real" bachelors degree,

they're all doing infinitely better than today's college graduates, and the reasons are many.

First, you are likely in WAY better financial shape than your college-graduating peers. I truly do get a laugh when I see a 21 year old auto-mechanic bringing down $40,000 a year with $25,000 in the bank who thinks he's somehow inferior to the "Hispanic Black Women's 15th Century Sculpture Lesbian Studies" graduate with $125,000 in debt, no employable skills, no savings, and an intolerable arrogance to boot. You have to understand, no matter what professors, teachers, counselors, or even your parents tell you, the sole point and purpose of a college education is to help increase your lifetime earnings. And the vast majority of kids today are majoring in hobbies, not skills. Therefore, unless you go to college for a real discipline such as engineering or the sciences, you are wasting your time (and money). And to compare yourself against a fool with a worthless piece of paper they spent four years and $75,000 on is laughable.

Second, you are not missing out on ANYTHING if you choose not to go to college, but instead figure out what you want to do in life first. The "college experience" and "college parties" are no different than any other party you'll attend in your 20's, minus the $87,000 tuition bill and crippling student loans attached to it. You aren't going to meet "smarter" people in college because now EVERYBODY goes to college, making it nothing more than High School v 2.0. It will be the exact same painful experience with the exact same idiots you endured in high school, but they'll all think they're really smart because "they're in college." And if you're worried you're going to miss out on the dating scene today in college? Think again. Women now get to choose from an increasingly effeminate, androgynous male student body epitomized by the infamous "Pajama Boy," while men get to choose from an increasingly hostile, angry, masculine, feminist female student body epitomized by the infamous "Trigglypuff." The hotter, sexier (not to mention, sane) people are out in the real world working real jobs, not in your mandatory freshman "Transgendered Women Male Sexual Woeisme Oppression Studies" class.

Finally, even though you are not going to college, you are light years ahead in terms of your education simply because you took the time to figure out first what you wanted to major in. The vast majority of your college-attending peers did not. And in failing to figure out what they wanted to major in first, they have condemned themselves to waste, **at minimum,** four years and $50,000 on a degree they're, frankly, never going to use.

Of course, at this moment in time, when your friends and peers are all graduating and partying, it seems the opposite. With all the great pomp and circumstance surrounding all the graduation ceremonies and graduation parties, it's hard as a degreeless 22 year old to think you're anything but a loser. But this is merely the bright flash of light before a bulb burns out because now, after this moment in time, the **nanosecond** after the graduation ceremony, your college-educated peers are for the first time in their lives leaving the K-college education system and entering...

the real world.

And the real world is NOT college.

Understand from K through college, from the ages of 5 to 25, you and all of your peers have lived in an artificial environment called school. You've lived in a bubble, protected from, even lied to about the realities of life. But what makes it worse is what you've been told was a "great accomplishment" or "excellence" in school is not the same in the real world.

Therefore, being:

the captain of the football team,
the best baton twirler in the marching band,
the hottest cheerleader who can do the most flips,
the best speller in the spelling bee,

or whatever other cornucopia of extra-curricular BS that passes for "excellence" in K-college, is ultimately worthless, pointless, useless, and meaningless in the real world.

In other words, school trains you to be good at school, not the real world. And unlike your college educated peers, you were at least smart enough to enter and explore the real world first, before you had to fork over $80,000 in tuition to extend this artificial "Lala-Land" of school an additional four years. So in reality, you are likely a full four years ahead of your college-graduating peers, not just in education, but work experience, personal finances, and employability.

They are in for a world of hurt.

Do NOT envy them.

CHAPTER 5
FAMILIAL HURDLES

Story #1

A client had finally realized that he didn't know what he wanted to study in college. He had completed his first year of community college, was disenchanted with the diversity/leftist/political indoctrination, and also made the astute observation he wasn't learning anything of employable value.

Logically, he made the decision he should postpone his education until the point in time he knew what he wanted to do, what he wanted to become, and therefore what he should study. He then withdrew from his college classes, opting instead to work during the daytime, only to find out that his decision to leave college prompted his parents to...

Cut off all financial support
Cut off all familial support
Lecture him about how he will achieve nothing in life, and
Kick him out of the house, forcing him to find his own lodging.

Story #2

Another client I had was in a quandary. He desperately wanted to escape the New York City ghetto and aspired to either join the military or major in engineering. He stayed out of trouble, avoided the gangs, got great grades in school, and was accepted into multiple engineering programs at multiple colleges.

There was just one problem.

His mother, completely dependent upon Section 8 housing, would receive a lower living allowance if her son left the home. Since she wouldn't be able to collect as much in Section 8 money, she guilt-tripped her son to stay at home, forcing him to forfeit his future and his life, all so she could collect a couple hundred shekels in extra cash from the taxpayer.

Story #3

And then there is, hands down, my most favorite client of them all.

An Iranian, originally sent here to become a doctor by his parents, found out he couldn't tolerate the site of blood and instead wished to pursue a career in chemical engineering. Despite this noble restructuring of priorities, his parents would have none of it. They cut him off completely, leaving him here in the US with absolutely no financial or familial support. Still he, quite heroically, decided to stay here and pursue his dreams where he's currently majoring in chemical engineering...

While living out of the Mercedes SUV his parents bought him
While also lifting weights at the local gym
While also showering there
While also working as a security guard to make ends meet and pay tuition.

Tragic, unfair, and unjust as these examples may be, they highlight the spectrum of responses you can expect from your family when you inform them you're not going to go to college like the rest of the lemmings, but instead will be going on a two year road trip to become a "Reconnaissance Man." Ideally, your parents will understand the wisdom in taking the time to figure things out, find out who you are, and what you want to become before you pursue a college education. But most won't which means you're likely going to have to confront them. And this may prove to be your biggest hurdle to becoming a Reconnaissance Man.

Ignorance or Abuse

In order to successfully get your parents to support you in your pursuit to become a Reconnaissance Man you'll have to be able to assess why they're against it. And here there are two general reasons why your parents will be against it. The first (and most common) reason is that they are ignorant about the economic realities of today's labor market, college degrees, and the education bubble. They're stuck in the 1960's and still think in order to be successful you MUST go to college. The second (and much worse) reason is they are abusive and controlling, and like the aforementioned clients above, don't really have your best interests at heart. They either view you as property to advance their own aims, want to use your success as a means to brag to other family members ("*you MUST become a doctor*"), or simply had you for purely religious reasons. Whatever the reason, they do not view you as a sentient individual with his/her own dreams, hopes, or even rights.

Once you find out whether it's ignorance or abuse, that will determine the argument you'll present to your parents for becoming a Reconnaissance Man. If your parents are merely ignorant about today's education bubble, a logical, honest, and empirical argument should convince them. Show them the actual data on student loans, the unemployment rate for people with college degrees, the *UNDER*employment rate for the same, the rate of tuition inflation, not to mention the thousands of horror stories where college graduates can't find jobs. Explain to them that you don't want to waste your time, your money, let alone **their** money on a degree or an education you just aren't sure of. Explain that you do indeed have a plan for your future and becoming a Reconnaissance Man is a vital first part of it. Even having them read the first few chapters of this book makes for a compelling argument that should convince most parents to support you. There is no guarantee they will condone your decision, but any reasonable, caring parent will see the wisdom in taking your time before rushing off to college.

The second instance is where your parents are abusive, and unfortunately, no amount of reasoning, evidence, logic, or empiricism will convince them because it will all fall on deaf ears. They have no interest in what's in your best interests, and will either cut funding, communication, or both if you don't do what they want you to do. Since their interests run contrary to yours, and they enforce their interests over yours via financing, you have only one choice – total self-reliance.

Self-Reliance

It amazed me in the 90's and continues to amaze me today just what a high percentage of 20 somethings and 30 somethings are financially dependent upon their parents. Getting help with rent, mommy paying the cell phone bill, daddy paying the car insurance, even parents who pay off their kids' student loans. You're 25 years old and you're ***still collecting an allowance and your mom buys you groceries???*** But whereas I envied my college peers who had a free ride through college, cars bought and paid for, free food, free healthcare, and free… well ….everything, there was one thing I did not envy.

They always needed permission from their parents to do anything.

And I continue to see this today with my clients at Asshole Consulting.

The 23 year old whose parents will cut him off financially if he doesn't return to school.
The 19 year old whose parents won't pay for her tuition because they disapproved of her major.
Even 30 year olds whose parents force them to attend church because they pay for the rent.

Here's a concept. Why don't you support yourself?

While 100% self-supportation is incredibly difficult, it is possible and it allows you 100% freedom to pursue your life as you please. Yes, you may have to eat ramen noodles. Yes, you may have to sleep on a couch for three years. And yes, you may not get to go on spring break in Florida every year. But you don't have to answer to your parents, major in what they tell you to, date who they want you to, or worship whichever god they command you to. In being 100% self-supporting you don't need them and can therefore do what you want.

Of course, becoming a 100% self-supporting adult fresh out of high school is difficult. Pay is low, you have no skills, and you may have to work multiple jobs. But to that I say...

Tough!

I worked full time while going to school fulltime. Lived in basements and slept on futons for 12 years to make ends meet. There was no partying or getting hammered. There was work, then school, and then some more work and school. Same thing with my friends I worked with in college. They'd work weekends, overnight shifts, holidays, and overtime all so they could support themselves and not have to answer to anybody. And if you ever think working a full time job and supporting yourself is tough, just remind yourself of our ostracized Iranian friend who lives out of his SUV and still manages to pull it off. There is no doubt that for an unfortunate number of you this will be the largest hurdle to becoming a Reconnaissance Man. But the problem is there is no other choice. You can forever be a slave to your parents, or you can live your own life.

Reconciling With Your Parents

The problem in cutting the cord from your parents so that you may live your own life is that you will likely alienate them at some level. In response they may kick you out of the household, ban you from ever revisiting them again, cut the financial purse strings, etc., and this obviously will take a psychological toll on you. Your family, the people who raised you, will potentially be gone forever, and whether controlling or not, they are your parents and you will miss them greatly on a psychological, emotional, and genetic level.

However, merely supporting yourself and telling your dad you're not going to become a surgeon, doesn't mean you abandon your parents or can't have a healthy relationship with them. You merely put them on hold. The current relationship you have with your parents is neither healthy nor acceptable. They need to realize and accept the fact that you're an independent person who has a right to live his/her life however you want. But until you can establish yourself financially and are no longer dependent upon them, you won't be able to take this commanding position and insist on such fair and equal treatment. You need to be able to go to your family, tell them "this is the life I'm pursuing" and if they disagree, that's perfectly fine, because you don't need them to survive. Your independence renders their acceptance moot. You merely disagree, have a difference of opinion, but you still love each other and are able to continue on in life.

To that end, and depending on the severity of how much your parents are alienated, you need to visit them and check in on them every once in a while. You need to test to see if they've come to accept your lifestyle AND to see if they will respect your decisions. You need to stop in on Thanksgiving and Christmas, have conversations, see if they've acknowledged you don't need them, but still choose to hang out with them as long as their treatment is fair. If it is, cool, you now have your family back WITH the added benefit of your parents' support and respect. If not, simply come back next year and the year after that until they come around. Because in the end, if you're self-reliant, they won't have a choice. It will be a reality they have to accept.

CHAPTER 6
WHERE TO RECON

After discussing all the philosophy, logistics, finance, psychology, and education behind becoming a Reconnaissance Man, there's only one question left – where do you recon? This is an important question not just because it's an obvious one, but because the United States is huge, and you simply don't have the time or money to waste on states like Delaware or Nebraska. Therefore, some kind of screening process needs to be employed to make our reconnaissance effective and expeditious.

Admittedly, however, there are some inherent drawbacks to any one particular vetting process. First, we are obviously only vetting the United States. Many of you may be curious about Thailand, China, Europe, or South America, which could also be viable and legitimate places to become a Reconnaissance Man. The only reason they are not in the scope of this book is simply because of the prohibitive expense of foreign travel. Second, there's no way to know you'd actually hate Delaware until you've actually been there. The perfect place with the perfect house with the perfect spouse and perfect job could very well be waiting for you in Delaware. It could in fact be your life destiny to live in Delaware. It's just statistically unlikely. Ergo, we have to focus our efforts on places that will likely provide us rewarding lives...not congestion, pollution, and high taxes. Finally, it's a guarantee I do not share the same tastes and preferences as everybody else. I personally loathe the cold, but you may love snowmobiling in it. This screening process is merely based on my past 10 years of personal adventuring, motorcycling riding, reconnaissance, and experience. Therefore, take this screening process with a pinch of salt. Just because a state doesn't make the "Top Ten" list, doesn't mean you shouldn't travel there if it piques your interest.

Methodology

The screening process we will use will eliminate states based on the following criteria:

- No Go Zones
- Climate
- Taxes/Economic Opportunity
- Beauty/Scenery/Outdoor Activity
- The Presence of a Major Metropolitan Center

Those states remaining will be further evaluated based on their pro's and con's. In the end, you will have *at minimum* a starting point to your journey to become a Reconnaissance Man. Ideally, however, somewhere in that list is where you'll be happiest and where you belong in life.

No Go Zones

To be blunt, some states in the United States just plain suck. There's just no godly reason to visit, let alone live there. This doesn't mean the people aren't nice or that there isn't *something* redeeming about them, it's just they're not states you should consider exploring unless you have a particular affinity for that state's particular character. You may like the absolute nothingness and solitude of North Dakota. You may like the sweltering heat of Alabama. And you might like the tornadoes of Oklahoma. But most people don't and so we can eliminate certain states immediately.

The largest group of states you can immediately check off your list are the plains states and the Midwest. Though fine people, and I'm sure the Nebraska Cornfest is a blast, these states offer little in terms of population, culture, and scenery. The next group you can eliminate are their southeastern cousins that also offer very little in the way of culture and scenery. Alabama, Mississippi, Louisiana, etc. All fine states, but not a place for aspiring and intrepid Reconnaissance Men. Finally, there are the east coast states who, frankly, live in a cocoon, never leave their home town, and think their states are the best. These are largely overpopulated, traffic-congested hell holes, and unless adjoining mountains or some other kind of scenery, they offer little to a young person's future and happiness.

After eliminating these states we are left with the following map:

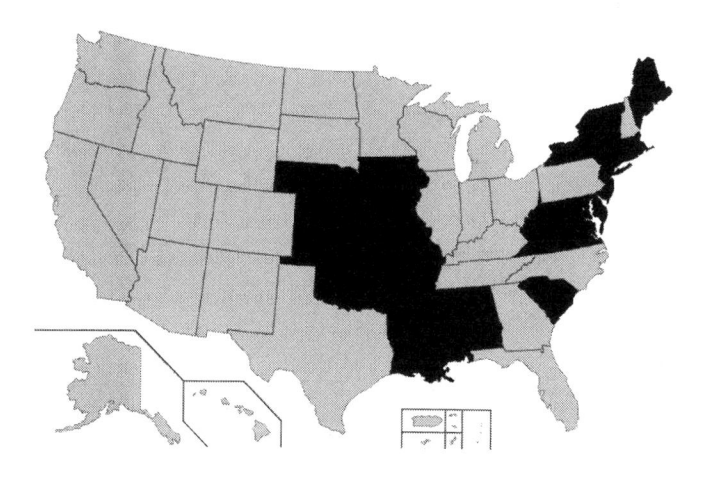

Climate

The next variable to consider is climate. Namely, do you have to endure harsh winters? Yes, many winter sports enthusiasts exist, but for all the fun you can have skiing, snowboarding, and ice-fishing you also get to deal with shoveling, heat bills, traffic jams, frost bite, hypothermia, and crippling blizzards. Besides, you can live in a warm state and fly to Colorado or Utah to go skiing. This eliminates most of the Upper Midwest and border-states with Canada.

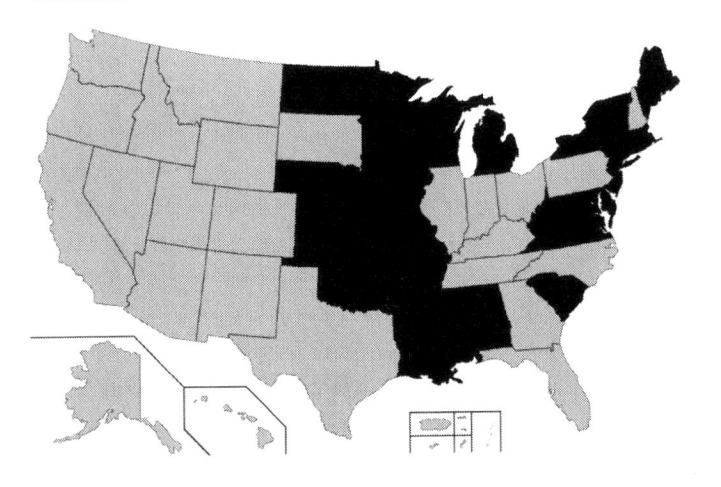

Taxes/Economic Opportunity

The third variable is economic opportunity, not just in terms of finding a job and having a successful career, but what percent of your hard earned money you get to keep. Not to introduce politics into this analysis, but take the leftist propaganda your teachers and professors told you about the evils of capitalism and financial success, toss it in the garbage, get your head out of your ass, and start thinking about your long term best interests. "Fun" and "glorious" as the media makes California or New York City seem, rent is prohibitively expensive, economic growth is lethargic, and your taxes can easily go above 50%. Worse, remember if you establish roots and a successful career in these states, it is infinitely more difficult to uproot yourself and leave for greener pastures. This doesn't mean you shouldn't visit California or New York City, but they offer NOTHING to any ambitious, hard-working young person, and should be taken off the list.

Another way to further pare down the list is to cut states that have LOCAL INCOME TAXES. This not only means you get to pay federal, state, AND local income taxes, but you often times have to fill out a THIRD INCOME TAX RETURN for the local government. There are some exceptions where only a few towns in a state actually charge a local income tax (notably Colorado), but we can now also eliminate the following states (if not eliminated already):

Alabama
California
Colorado*
Delaware
Indiana
Iowa
Kansas
Kentucky
Maryland
Michigan
Missouri
New Jersey
New York
Ohio
Oregon
Pennsylvania
West Virginia

Leaving us with the following map:

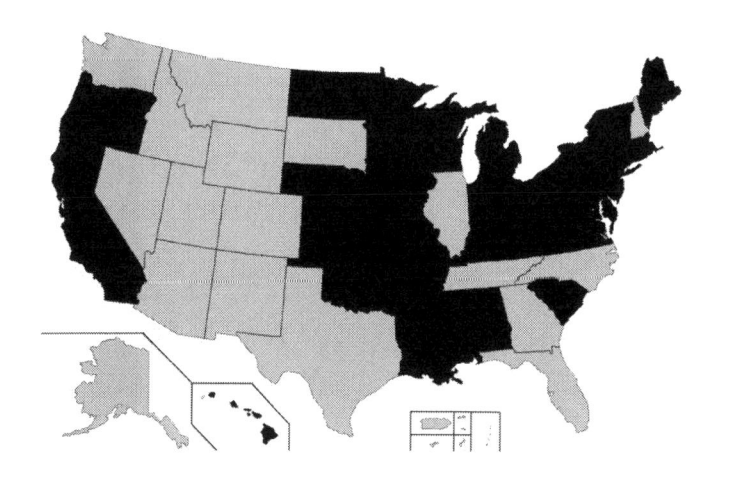

Beauty/Scenery/Outdoor Activity

The fourth variable is whether there is scenery and beauty, and therefore some form of outdoor activity for you to enjoy. You can't be stuck looking at the same wheat fields every day in Minot, North Dakota just as you can't be stuck seeing the same traffic jam in Baltimore, Maryland. Like architecture you need to see beauty and variety. However, scenery and beauty also play a role in your physical and mental health because you need to be outdoors enjoying life. Yes, you may like playing video games, yes you may like watching sportsball, but to live a full life you need a massive and outdoor playground in your back yard that you can explore and thoroughly enjoy.

Here, however, we have to start splitting states up into zones because rarely is an entire state "scenic." South Dakota for example is 95% flat, boring nothingness, until you get to the Black Hills on its far west side. Illinois has nothing to offer, bar some architecture and culture in Chicago. And New Mexico is a trailer trash dump where people leave garbage in their front yards until you get north of Santa Fe. Carving out these blighted areas from different states we further trim our map down to this:

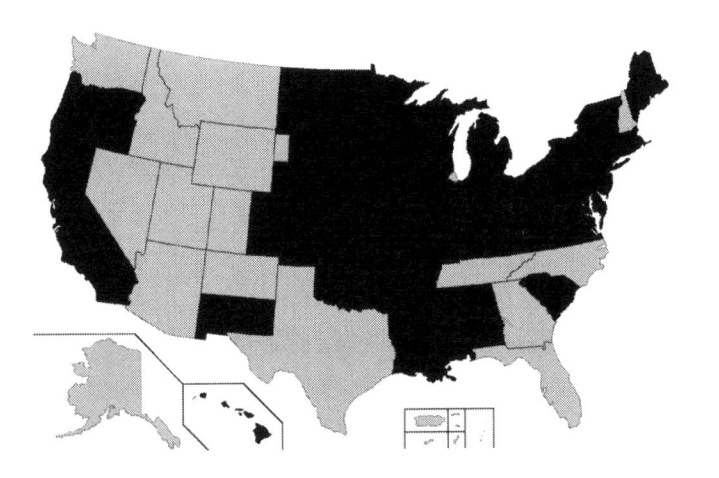

The Presence of a Major Metropolitan Area

The final variable will be one of convenience and culture as having a major (or even moderate) metro area improves your life in terms of convenience, employment, entertainment, culture, social life, and dating. You may want to be a hermit, living in the outer hinterlands of Wyoming, but driving 200 miles to the nearest Wal-Mart, grocery store, let alone cell phone tower is not only tiring, but prohibitively expensive both in terms of gas and time. This doesn't mean you have to live in downtown Denver, a walk's distance from the Boettcher Symphony Hall, but within an acceptable radius of a city where you can find employment, high speed internet, a grocer, and perhaps somebody to date.

Mapping this is nearly impossible as there's too many areas in too many states that graphing it would be too obtuse. Besides, most remaining states do have major metro areas. Utah has Salt Lake City. Colorado has Denver. Arizona has Phoenix. And Texas has a ton of large metro areas. But there is one state that does not have a major metro area and is one you want to avoid with all of your might – Wyoming.

Wyoming, though physically beautiful, is a backwards and utterly contemptable state. It's low population not only makes it sparse, lacking in infrastructure, and culture, but what culture you do find is the purest form of trailer trash that ever existed. Meth, alcohol, STD's, and teenage pregnancy are the national past times of towns like Casper, Gillette, and Laramie, and I would not recommend traveling through these "towns" without a gun. Still, there are some must-visit gems in Wyoming such as Yellowstone National Park, Buffalo, Sheridan, and Jackson. These are largely found in the upper and western quadrants of the state and could, for a tolerant and hearty few, potentially be places to live. However, the remaining three-quarters of the state is an absolute No Go Zone for anybody with an ounce of taste, reason, and self-respect.

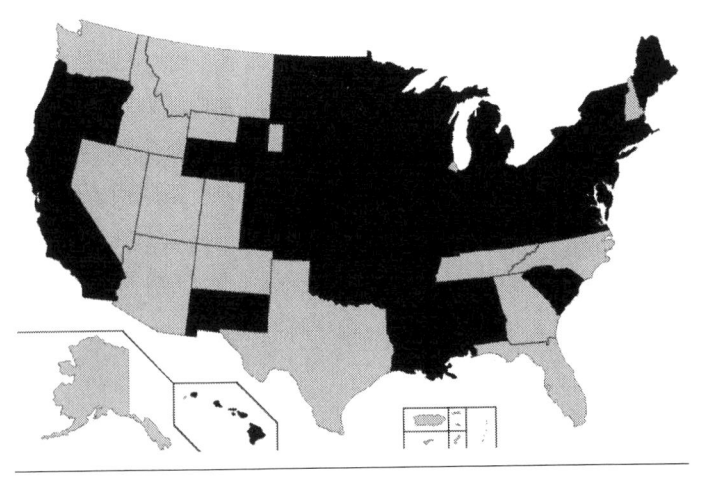

Qualifying States

After adjusting for No Go Zones, climate, economic opportunity, scenery, and metropolitan areas, there are 16 states that remain and should be the focus of your reconnaissance. Again, this doesn't mean you shouldn't visit Oregon or California (both states are very beautiful and offer excellent adventuring) or that you shouldn't visit New York City or Boston. But when it comes to plotting and planning the initial stages of your reconnaissance these are the states where your focus should be.

<u>Washington</u>

Washington is actually quite a diverse state when it comes to scenery - mountains, lakes, plains, even high-desert. It offers everything a state can, ranging from fishing to mountaineering to a major cosmopolitan metropolitan area – Seattle. It also has the enviable advantage of having no personal income taxes. The entire state is worth exploring, everything from Spokane to Seattle. The only drawback, however, is the town of Seattle itself.

It's very crowded, pinched between the Cascade Mountains and Puget Sound, resulting in some of the worst traffic the US has to offer. The town is also very "progressive" which not only means increased local taxes, but it has also become home to some of the worst and most annoying panhandlers. Much of this can be ameliorated by simply not living in Seattle or the county in which it sits, King County. But in terms of reconnaissance both the city of Seattle and the State of Washington are absolute musts.

Idaho

Idaho is a very beautiful, but very sparsely populated state. The most scenic parts of Idaho run along its Montana and Wyoming borders with the jagged Bitterroot Mountains and their trout-packed rivers. Its panhandle includes two must-see towns along the I-90 interstate –Wallace and Coeur d'Alene - but most of the state is mountainous and pock-marked with picturesque mountain towns anyway. The southern end of Idaho, however, is relatively desolate as it turns into the Nevadan desert. However, two major metros – Boise and Twin Falls – are in the area and make for good "base camps" when reconnoitering Idaho.

(The Bitterroot Mountains from the top of Trapper Peak looking into Idaho)

(Lake Coeur d'Alene in Idaho)

Montana

Montana is a great place to visit…during summer. Because of its northern latitude and high altitude bitter winters and harsh snow storms are the norm. Glacier National Park is a park every person should visit, but you often times have to wait until July for its mountain passes to melt of snow. Particularly hearty Reconnaissance Men will like Montana due to its hiking, rafting, fishing, hunting, vast expanses, and rugged individualist culture. But if you don't like the cold, insist on a motorcycle riding season longer than 4 months, or want more culture than what its largest city (Billings) has to offer, you may simply wish to thoroughly visit this otherwise fine state.

(Glacier National Park, Montana)

Nevada

Nevada consists of two towns with a whole lot of nothingness in between – Las Vegas and Reno. And between those two towns the only one that really matters is Las Vegas.

Though largely nothing but desert, Las Vegas alone makes the State of Nevada not only a must-visit, but a very likely contender for a place to plant roots. Because of Vegas, Nevada has no personal income taxes, its economy is recession proof as they come, entertainment abounds, there's a ton of young people, flights are dirt cheap, and you can get every luxury in the world in what is arguably the world's most famous city.

But the real selling point of Las Vegas is its general centrality to the United States West. Within a four hour radius you can visit LA, the Pacific Ocean, the Grand Canyon, Zion National Park, Bryce Canyon National Park, Monument Valley, Hoover Dam, Lake Mead, Lake Havasu, Charleston Peak, Death Valley, Phoenix, San Diego, and the Grand Escalante. And this says nothing of the score of local, state, and regional parks just outside Las Vegas' city limits.

Las Vegas is so ideal for reconnaissance, I would strongly recommend you start there, making it a base of operations, and hitting all the other major towns and landmarks in a 400 mile radius. The only drawback is that it gets hotter than hell there during the summer which may cause some logistical problems. Still, spending your Christmas breaks in the warm climes of Vegas and exploring the surrounding area is a wise investment of your time.

(Red Rocks State Park with Las Vegas in the background. Vegas is NOT just gambling and casinos!)

Utah

Utah is quite simply the most beautiful state you will ever find. It has deserts, it has snow-capped mountains, it has salt flats, it has arches, it has forests, and it has the world's most incomprehensibly beautiful canyons. You cannot leave this planet without at least visiting Zion and Canyonlands National Parks. Unfortunately, it has a slight sociological drawback due to its Mormon founding. It's a very religious state and therefore has some laws regarding curfews, alcohol, and bars that more secular people might find restrictive and annoying.

Still, if you're not the partying type, Utah has several towns that every Reconnaissance Man should visit, and maybe even consider settling down in. Salt Lake City is a large, modern metropolitan area offering all the amenities of a major city. It is also surrounded by three mountain ranges and the Great Salt Lake making for spectacular views (and unlimited outdoor activities). St. George is a sizeable town with all the modern day infrastructure you need, and although nothing fancy it is situated just outside Zion National Park and 90 minutes from Las Vegas. But if you ever win the lottery and don't mind slow-driving, aging trust-funders, Moab is hands down a town you want to consider living in. Though not large, it is smack dab in the most beautiful part of Utah, sitting at the intersection of Canyonlands National Park, Arches National Park, the Colorado, and Green Rivers. The scenery is so dense and concentrated you have world-class hiking, rock climbing, mountain biking, fishing, four-wheeling, motorcycling, white water rafting, and camping all within a mere 15 mile radius of town. Do not be surprised, however, if a hotel room runs you $300 a night.

(Dead Horse Point in Moab, Utah)

(Island in the Sky, Canyonlands National Park, Utah)

(Highway 128 alongside the Colorado River just outside Moab, Utah)

(Temple of Sinawava, Zion National Park, Utah)

Colorado

If I were to do it all over again, the nano-second I graduated from high school I would have moved to Denver, Colorado. The reasons are many. First, it sits at the base of the Rocky Mountains giving you 30 minutes access to some of the best mountain climbing in the United States. Second, it is a large city offering not just the comforts of big-city living, but plenty of quality schools. I could have lived there for a year, gained residency, and thus, paid in-state tuition for one of these quality schools. Third, it was, and still is, growing. More and more people are moving to Colorado for its standard of living, it's outdoor activities, and its mild climate. It would have been much easier to find a job and establish a career in a town that has grown by 23% since 2000 than Minneapolis, which has grown only by 7%. And finally, like Utah, it simply has everything. Mountains, deserts, canyons, rivers, forests, and fossils. All one has to do is drive around the towns of Boulder and Golden on a nice summer day and see Coloradans playing on this big and massive adult playground. You will see hang gliders, mountain climbers, cyclists, white water rafters, hikers, fishers, gold-panners, runners, race car drivers, and people just sitting there smiling because they live there and you don't.

However, Denver is not the only town in Colorado worth visiting. Since Colorado is one of the more densely populated western states there are other towns large enough to support a modern lifestyle. If you like the mountains, but don't like crowds, towns like Fort Collins, Loveland, Colorado Springs, and Pueblo are all along the I-25 corridor conveniently located at the foothills of the Rockies, but without the Denver-esque population. Ski-resorts such as Aspen, Breckenridge, Steamboat, and Telluride are options, especially for avid snowboarders and skiers, but you typically need a ton of money to live in these towns. And then there are more of the classical "Wild West towns" of Grand Junction, Cortez, and Durango. These are on the southwest side of the Rockies and are therefore warmer during winter. This provides for longer hiking, rafting, cycling, and climbing seasons.

The only real drawback Colorado has is that it allows its local governments to implement an income tax. Thankfully, only three towns have implemented one – Denver, Aurora, and Greenwood. Still, it's not so much the cost of the local income tax (it's so low it amounts to about $4 per month), it's the annoyance of having to pay it. Still, as long as you live outside of these towns AND do not conduct significant business within them, you can avoid this petty and bothersome tax.

(There is snow in Colorado in June)

Arizona

Arizona would be an ideal contender for planting roots if it wasn't the hottest state in the country. For nine months a year it is gorgeous, but unless you live in Flagstaff, the summer months are practically unbearable. Your air-conditioning can cost over $300 a month, it's not uncommon to see the mercury never drop below 100, and you're basically scurrying from one air-conditioned building to another with intermittent stops in air-conditioned cars. But if you can handle the heat, Arizona is a great place to consider living in, as well as a must for conducting reconnaissance.

First, you have scenery almost as beautiful as Utah. There is the Grand Canyon, the Apache Trail, Lake Powell, the Vermillion Cliffs, Humphrey's Peak, and the Superstition Mountains. The state is also dotted with picturesque towns such as Bisbee, Carefree, Wickenburg, Prescott, Sedona, Jerome, and if you like burrows, Oatman. But arguably the main selling point of Arizona is its largest town, Phoenix. Once again it is a major metropolitan area that provides for every possible convenience and luxury you could want. But it also has an interesting landscape that gives it a very Colorado feel. It has mountains in the middle of town. This leads to a young (and old) vibrant outdoor hiking community, not to mention, sexier people.

(Overlooking the Phoenix Valley from Black Mountain, in Care Free, Arizona)

(Canyon Lake on the Apache Trail outside Phoenix, Arizona)

New Mexico

New Mexico, in short, is a wannabe Arizona. It has a wannabe Phoenix (Albuquerque). It has a wannabe Sedona (Santa Fe). It has a wannabe Flagstaff (Taus). And it has wannabe cops (a speed trap in the city of Elida which I strongly recommend you avoid). The rest of the state is more or less a run-down dump as people really do leave trash in their yards, buildings in disrepair, and nobody seems to care about picking up the joint. With Arizona being a vastly superior state and right next door, there's really no reason to live in New Mexico, but you may want to take a drive through it out of boredom.

South Dakota

Like Utah and Colorado, South Dakota is one of my favorite places to visit and is currently vying with Las Vegas as the place I will inevitably retire to. However, there is only a small section of South Dakota worth visiting and that is the "Black Hills" region which is located in the south west quadrant of the state.

The Black Hills is a small, but beautiful mountain range that is home to Mount Rushmore, Deadwood, and Sturgis. Scattered across the region are small former mining towns-turned-tourist traps, but the two largest cities (Spearfish and Rapid City) are large enough to host two Wal-Marts, significant downtown centers, a drive-in theater, and even a cigar lounge. The area is large and diverse enough that you can fish, hike, climb, hunt, camp, boat, etc., but has the added benefit of being in a "banana belt." This banana belt makes the region warmer than its surrounding area, resulting in mild winters and wonderful summers.

If this wasn't good enough, immediately to the east of the Black Hills is Badlands National Park. This is a unique park full of "badland formations," spectacular layers of strata, fossils, ghost towns, buffalo, and truly amazing views which mandate your attendance. This park, when combined with all the Black Hills has to offer, makes this region of South Dakota a required part of your reconnaissance.

(The Black Hills of South Dakota)

Texas

With its open ranges, Wild West history, and vast expanses of land, Texas, as American as it may be, is really only quite average in terms of a place to explore and potentially live. There are certainly proud Texans who would disagree, but Texas is basically a very large, dry, semi-mountainous, quasi-desert with very large cities and no taxes. This is great if you're looking to get an education or start a career. Texas is full of large, growing towns like Dallas, Austin Houston, and San Antonio. And Texas is also a fine state to raise a family. But aside from size, its landscape and cities don't really stand out from the rest of their American counterparts. Its mountains aren't as high as Colorado's. Its desert isn't as pretty as Arizona's. Its forests aren't as lush as Montana's. And its cities aren't as big or cultured as Chicago.

The one thing Texas does have going for it is its culture. This is not so much something you can see or visit as much as it's something you'll experience over time. Texans are proud, they are pro-business, they are for individuality, and they are for freedom. You can't shoot a gun, roast a pig, smoke a cigar, race cars, and drink Jack Daniels all on a Sunday in New York City. But you sure as hell can do all that and more in Texas. The larger point is that Texas and its major towns are certainly worth a visit, but its main selling point won't be the scenery. It will be its culture. But to understand and appreciate this culture, you can't be zooming across Texas as you try to recon the entire state, not to mention New Mexico and Arizona, all in a two week period. You need to take your time in Texas, spending at least a week in each major town, which may make Texas its own reconnaissance mission.

(Sunset 50 miles east of Van Horn, Texas)

Tennessee

Tennessee is one of the few eastern states to make the list simply because it's beautiful, it has culture, it has no income taxes, and a young man/woman can do quite well there. Its eastern quarter is ensconced in the Smoky Mountains providing for numerous outdoor activities. It has two large metropolitan areas, one with a rich river culture (Memphis) and another with an even richer music/country culture (Nashville). It has smaller towns like Chattanooga and Knoxville in case you don't like the big city. It's below the Mason Dixon line so its winters are very mild. And in 2016 they got rid of all forms of personal income taxes.

There are no real major drawbacks to Tennessee, bar its location which more or less relegates you to the south east. This isn't to say states south of the Ohio valley aren't fun to explore, but nobody ever said *"Hot diggity, I can't wait to do that road trip to Alabama!"* This makes Tennessee much like Texas in that it may be more of a suitable place to go to college, start a career, and raise a family than one to be adventuring about, summiting peaks, crossing deserts, and rafting rivers.

North Carolina

Take Tennessee, add the benefit of having access to the Atlantic Ocean, minus the benefit of no state income taxes, flip it on its eastern border and you have North Carolina. Like Tennessee, North Carolina has a mild climate, growing economy, scenic mountains, plus access to the Atlantic Ocean. It unfortunately has state income taxes, but this economic drawback is countered by the town of Raleigh-Durham which boasts some great colleges and a booming technology sector. Again, like Tennessee and Texas, North Carolina is probably more suited for pursuing a career and raising a family than adventuring up 14,000 foot mountains and racing a motorcycle across the Wild West. But North Carolina's remote and mountainous western region should provide you a bit of that pioneering spirit.

Georgia

The only reason Georgia makes the list is because of its largest city, Atlanta. It's crowded, hot, and has atrocious traffic, but Atlanta offers a unique opportunity, especially to those aspiring Reconnaissance Men stuck in towns like Philadelphia, New York, Baltimore, Detroit, Chicago, Cleveland, Boston, and DC.

A place to escape.

The truth is most people who grew up and live in the large towns of the northeastern United States live in a bubble. Their parents, teachers, local community leaders, etc., make it seem that you can never leave Philly. Media, television, and the movies fool youth into thinking New York City is the center of the universe. And if you want to get around Baltimore or DC, you can only use the bus or the train. Never a car.

This unconsciously and unintentionally traps young people in these northeastern towns. Without a car they can't just pick up and leave. And since they never leave, they are repeatedly and constantly mentally reinforced to believe they can ONLY live in the big city. This predisposes them to have a hesitation, even a fear of leaving the "big city" for the "Wild West" because *"Thar be monsters out thar!!!"* So they languish away in these dying, leftist, east coast towns, enduring bitter winters, no economic opportunity, high taxes, living at home, and high living costs.

But then there's Atlanta.

Though not an east coast megalopolis, it is large enough to provide the comforts of a large city. It's east of the Mississippi so its culture is not too unlike that of the north east. It's warm so you'll never experience the hellish snow totals Boston did in the winter of 2014-2015. And unlike its stagnant northeastern rust belt counterparts, its economy is growing, not dying.

In other words, Atlanta is a great alternative for east coast Reconnaissance Men who either have no interest in, or are too intimidated by, visiting and exploring America's West. It's a great compromising first step that will allow you to "Escape from New York" and try your hand at a difficult culture that is not so drastically different it sends you running back to your dying east coast town. Summers are, of course, unbearably hot, and it certainly isn't a minor step you're taking by moving 900 miles away. But if you want to try your hand at something different and escape the malaise and lack of opportunity large east coast towns offer their youth, Atlanta is a great town to reconnoiter.

Florida

Florida is the wild card of the reconnaissance states because of various economic, demographic, and sociological forces. First, it has no personal income taxes and therefore attracts a ton of rich people. Second, you have a ton of old people moving there to retire. Third, while you'd think all the old people would make Florida "Dullsville," you have a large and bustling Latino culture that breathes new and different life into it. Fourth, it's surrounded by water resulting in the largest marine/boating/beach-partying culture in the United States. And fifth, just to mix things up even more, Disney has a huge theme park in the middle of the state. Florida is the epitome of a bustling, booming, economy which mandates you at least spend one week reconnoitering the state.

There's just three problems with Florida.

One, it's an inconveniently located peninsula. Unless you have a boat, you are stuck on a peninsula that is as far away from the rest of the country as possible, bar Alaska. This means traveling to other parts of the country will prove costly both in terms of time and money. Flights are long, road trips are longer, and even after driving seven hours straight you'll still be stuck in either Alabama, Mississippi, Georgia, or South Carolina. In other words, unless you have a large travel budget, you're going to be stuck there.

Two, its terrain is uniformly flat. Sugarloaf "Mountain" stands at 312 feet and is the highest peak in Florida. This means your outdoor activity and life will have to revolve around the water or standard activities such as running, cycling, volleyball, etc. There's no places to hike, there's no places to explore, there's no canyons to raft. You basically can exercise, fish, boat, or (as most Floridians do) eat.

Third, it's over-populated. Since Florida is a peninsula and its population is booming, you can have traffic jams at 2AM on a Sunday morning. This is not a major problem for most Floridians in that they more or less stay put in their local town. But if you are any kind of adventuring type, traffic is increasingly becoming a deal-breaking problem.

When you combine these problems, Florida essentially turns into one huge nightclub. Once you go there, to enjoy it, you have to stay there. And after a while eating at the same chain restaurants, smoking at the same cigar lounges, dancing at the same salsa clubs will get boring. You can certainly move to another part of the night club, but Florida is so uniform it's the same chain restaurants, same type of culture, and same people that are always there. If you want a real change, you'll have to leave the peninsula.

All these drawbacks aside, keep in mind I very much enjoy Florida. It boasts many major cosmopolitan cities such as Miami, St. Petersburg, Tampa, Jacksonville, and Fort Myers. It has the Florida Keys in case you are looking to escape the bustling city and want a Jimmy Buffett relaxed island lifestyle. Its Latino culture is a godsend with cigars, food, salsa dancing, and gorgeous women. And the town of Daytona hosts not only Spring Break, but two separate motorcycle rallies. It's a great place to escape winter, but its homogeneity gets boring after a couple months.

(Downtown St. Petersburg from the Vinoy docks)

New Hampshire

New Hampshire is the only New England state that qualified for reconnaissance simply for one reason – it isn't a socialist state like the rest of New England. Unlike New York, Massachusetts, Connecticut, and its twin brother, Vermont, New Hampshire has remained a bastion of low taxes, freedom, and economic growth. New Hampshire also has an additional advantage most other reconnaissance states don't and that is you can easily enjoy what New England has to offer without paying the egregious taxes. The Adirondacks of New York, the lakes of Maine, the fall leaves of Vermont, the American history of Boston, and the hustle and bustle of New York, all within a half day's drive, and all at New Hampshire taxpayer prices. This, combined with its mountainous interior and access to the Atlantic Ocean means New Hampshire is not only worth visiting, but also a viable candidate for long term residency.

The only drawback New Hampshire has is, like Florida, it's remotely located in the far north eastern part of the country making travel to the rest of the country time-consuming and costly. You won't be completely stranded from culture, however, since

Boston is a mere hour's drive away, but if you ever wanted to escape New England, road tripping to Denver or flying to Seattle will prove particularly cumbersome.

Alaska

Alaska is so beautiful not only is it a must for all aspiring Reconnaissance Men, it is a state that you will have to dedicate an entire season of reconnaissance to if you wish to do it justice. Alaska is simply too large, too different, and offers too much that a slapdash, two week run-through just won't cut it. Unfortunately, Alaska is even more remote than New Hampshire or Florida, resulting in some logistical problems. It's going to take time and money to get there. And it's going to take even more time and money to stay there. You will have to travel vast expanses of road, driving up your fuel expense, and if you really want to experience Alaska you'll need to charter "puddle jumpers" (small planes) as a lot of the state is inaccessible by car. Sadly, this postpones Alaska for most Reconnaissance Men until the point in time we make enough money to afford it. But like Vegas you ***need to do it.***

The major problem facing Alaska, however, is not the logistics or costs it's going to take you to get out there. It's the population and climate. Like Montana, Alaska is great to visit during summer. But come winter unless you are in Anchorage or Ketchikan, it's not only prohibitively cold, but the lack of sun is depressing. This harsh climate has ensured only the heartiest and smallest of a population resides in Alaska, resulting in a very small economy that is narrowly focused on natural resources and tourism. These factors make planting roots in Alaska an option for only a very rare few, but it is still a must-visit for every Reconnaissance Man.

(Entering the US border at Hyder, Alaska)

Must Visits

Even though we whittled our reconnaissance list down to 16 states, these states account for over 2/3rds the land mass of the US. There are literally thousands of different things to see in this million square mile area and frankly, you don't have the life expectancy to see them all. Therefore to ensure you don't miss out on any of the major landmarks, parks, etc., compiled below is a list of must-visit locations in the United States (and an optional one in Canada).

Beartooth Pass/Chief Joseph's Highway

Located on the border between Wyoming and Montana, "Beartooth Pass" is one of the highest passes in the United States. This is part of a mountain road system called "Chief Joseph Highway" that you can pick up just north of Cody, Wyoming. Unless you drive to Alaska you are unlikely to see such dramatic mountain peaks, dramatic switchbacks, or drops. I also recommend visiting Cooke City, Montana while you're there.

(Beartooth Pass straddling the Wyoming and Montana border on Highway 212)

Canyonlands/Arches/Highway 128

Canyonlands National Park, Arches National Park, and the scenic route of Highway 128 are conveniently located all within a 10 mile radius of Moab, Utah. All three can be done in a day and you are unlikely to see such views with such convenience anywhere else in the world. Canyonlands is, however, a MASSIVE park with three completely different sections. It is by far my favorite national park, and I recommend spending at least a week in that park alone.

Zion and Bryce National Parks

Like Canyonlands and Arches National Parks, Zion and Bryce are conveniently located near each other so you can drive through them both in a day. However, you will not want a mere fly-by of these parks, as their beauty demands you explore them more thoroughly. Two must-hikes are Angel's Landing and the Temple of Sinawava, both of which are located in Zion. While any hike in Bryce will not go unrewarded.

(The pinnacle view from Angel's Landing in Zion National Park)

Monument Valley

Also located in Utah, Monument Valley boats the iconic cliffs that jut out of the otherwise flat desert on the Navajo Indian Reservation. Though considerably out of the way, the drive along Highway 163 also includes "Mexican Hat" and some other amazing formations outside the town of Bluff, Utah. If you have a full day, you can also manage to get in "Four Corners" which is both overpriced and underwhelming, but you'll at least have bragging rights that you've seen it.

(Monument Valley about where Forrest Gump stopped running)

Dinosaur National Monument

Dinosaur National Monument straddles the border between Utah and Colorado just outside Vernal, Utah. Though noted for its massive dinosaur find, it also has amazing canyons carved out by the Green River (which inevitably flows south and creates the canyons in Canyonlands National Park). This not only allows for some spectacular hiking, but rafting and a beautiful drive up Highway 191 to the Flaming Gorge Dam.

The Grand Canyon

Though so popular it's cliché, the Grand Canyon is something everybody must see before they die. Even if you don't hike it, just seeing it is worth the trip. However, it is inconveniently located, requiring a 90 minute drive north of the Interstate. Complicating matters further, the weather is actually quite fickle and you will want to check in advance before driving out there. I've now had ***three trips*** to the Grand Canyon thwarted by rain, ice, and (mockingly so) a complete fog out.

(The Grand Canyon, ironically, fogged out)

Canyon of the Ancients

When it comes to the town of Cortez, Colorado you will have a choice. You can spend $25 and an extra hour on the road to visit Mesa Verde National Park, or you can just drive out west for 10 minutes, pull your car over, and hike Canyon of the Ancients for free. The attraction for both parks are the same – ancient Ute Indian dwellings. But Canyon of the Ancients is not only more convenient, scenic, and free, it also has infinitely more ancient adobe dwellings you can see up close and personal. Do NOT pass up this free opportunity if you enjoy history and archeology!

(Free entrance to Canyon of the Ancients just outside Cortez, Colorado)

(One of many ancient adobe dwellings you will see in Canyon of the Ancients)

The Apache Trail

Located to the west of Phoenix, the Apache Trail is a winding, beautiful, drive through the jagged Superstition Mountains. While cowards will turn around at the tourist trap of "Tortilla Flats," real Reconnaissance Men will continue onto Fish Creek Hill where the road drops down a white-knuckling, 1,500 feet. One slip up and you will die. There is no reason to continue onto Roosevelt Lake, so once you navigate to the bottom of Fish Creek Hill, it's time to turn around and do it all over again going up.

Tensleep Canyon

Tensleep Canyon is on the south west side of the Big Horn mountain range in northern Wyoming. The roughly one hour drive between Tensleep and Buffalo is scenic enough itself, but the canyon will leave you speechless. Since you will already be on Highway 16 it behooves you to drive down "Crazy Woman Canyon Road" and then go north into Buffalo, Wyoming. There you will find one of my favorite bars, "The Occidental," which conveniently also happens to be a must.

(Tensleep Canyon looking upstream)

Spearfish Canyon

Located just south of Spearfish, South Dakota, the Spearfish Canyon follows Spearfish Creek for 20 miles into the Black Hills. Though not as deep as Tensleep Canyon it is just as spectacular because of its steeper and moss-colored cliffs. Upon reaching Cheyenne Crossing it is advisable to take Highway 85 north into the towns of Lead and Deadwood which not only have casinos and a ton of history, but are where Wild Bill Hickok and Calamity Jane are buried. The cigar lounge in Deadwood is also recommended.

(Spearfish Canyon from the top. Crow Peak is in the background)

Mount Rushmore

Like the Grand Canyon, Mount Rushmore is also a stereotypical must. There really isn't much else to do but look at it, so if you find yourself bored in about 10 minutes, stop feeling compelled and leave. Do be aware there is a place you can view Mount Rushmore for free just outside Keystone, South Dakota, but because everybody pulls over there to view it, accidents occur regularly.

Harney's Peak/Needles Highway/Cathedral Spires

As Harney's peak is the highest peak in the Black Hills it is a must that you hike it. You will pay a fee to enter by Sylvan Lake, park your vehicle, and look for Trailhead #9. This will lead you to Harney's Peak which will give you the best view of the Black Hills possible. However, since you are in the heart of the Black Hills, if you take the alternative route back (Trail Heads #3 to #4) you can see other spectacular views, notably the Cathedral Spires. The entire hike is no more than eight miles roundtrip and can easily be done in under four hours. If you have the time, I'd also advise doing the Sunday Gulch hike as well.

After completing your hike/s you will want to drive a different route back so you can see the Needles Highway. Take Highway 87 East and you will almost immediately hit The Needles which consists of 180 degree pin turns, switchbacks, and narrow tunnels. Continue to Route 753 (aka South Playhouse Road) where you will take a left, continuing to 16A where you will go left again. This will take you to the Iron Mountain Look Out which is a lesser known vista, as well as some amazing hairpin turns before re-entering Keystone.

(Harney's Peak at sunset, taken from the opposing Sylvan's Peak)

Badlands National Park

Roughly an hour east of the Black Hills is Badlands National Park. And though you may be exhausted from your travels in the Black Hills, you should put just as much energy into exploring the Badlands as you did the Black Hills.

The Badlands consist of three areas or "units." The North Unit, the Stronghold Unit, and the Palmer Creek Unit. Accessing the Palmer Creek Unit requires getting permission from the local landowners on the Indian Reservation. The issue is not that they won't give you permission, but good luck finding the owner in this otherwise barren and unpopulated wasteland. The Stronghold Unit you can access easily from Indian Highway 2, but lacks roads, trails, and landmarks which makes it difficult and dangerous to navigate. The Northern Unit, however, is not just the most popular, but it is also the most scenic part of the park, easily accessible from the interstate. This allows you to view the park in most of its glory from the comforts of a car, but because the main road is easily identifiable atop the crescent shaped ridge that forms the park, you can easily hike the entire Northern Unit without much chance of getting lost.

Finally, there are a ton of amazing fossils found every year in the Badlands. Ammonites, brontotheres, oreodonts, ancient horses. And while it's unlikely you'll happen across one, you absolutely must stop in at the visitors center where you can see paleontologists cut, clean, and prepare fossils that were found in the field.

(The vast expanses of the South Dakota Badlands)

Banff/Jasper/Lake Louise/ Highway 93

Though not part of the United States, if you happen to be traveling to Alaska or are in Canada, it is mandatory you drive the Highway 93 Route from Banff National Park to Jasper National Park. These parks alone are worth a detour, but there is no drive that compares to what you will see along Highway 93. While every view is a picture, stopping in at Lake Louise and Athabasca Glacier are musts. I'd even recommend spending the extra money to stay at the lodge at Lake Louise.

(Lake Louise)

(A "typical" view along Highway 93)

Las Vegas

Las Vegas, as previously mentioned, is not only where I recommend you start your reconnaissance, but is a viable candidate to plant roots. However, whether it is part of a larger reconnaissance plan, or just a one-time visit, every young person must visit Las Vegas at least once. Therefore, if you can only afford a weekend trip, go to Las Vegas because it will give you the most bang for your reconnaissance buck.

However, before you visit Vegas remember why you are going there. You are NOT going there to gamble. You are not going there to see shows. And you sure as hell aren't going there for the "bunny or stud ranches." You are going there to conduct reconnaissance. This means you can skip the casinos and all the touristy stuff, and instead explore the city itself and the surrounding area.

Denver

Denver is where I would have gone to college if I were to do it all over again. And though that opportunity has passed, Denver still remains one of my favorite towns because it offers everything a

Reconnaissance Man could want. Access to every form of outdoor activity and landscape possible. A growing economy. A mild climate. Good looking people. All with the conveniences, luxuries, and technologies a major city offers. Regardless of age, like Vegas, you need to visit Denver.

North Side Chicago

If you pay attention to the map, you'll notice on the bottom left side of Lake Michigan there's a small gray spot that you should visit. That gray spot is Chicago. And not just any part of Chicago. The **north side** of Chicago.

Though seemingly failing the criteria we used to determine where to recon, the north side of Chicago is still a must for every young man and woman. I wouldn't live there if you paid me, but the culture in terms of music, architecture, food, and above all else, friendly people mandate you visit this part of town. It will not only give you an experience of what it's like to live in a truly major city, but will show you what humanity is capable of in terms of engineering, architecture, art, music, culinary, and every other facet of human accomplishment. To that end I recommend you do a "Ferris Bueller's Day Off" in Chicago, albeit adjusted for today's time:

Drive Lake Shore Drive at night.
Listen to jazz at The Green Mill.
Walk along the Gold Coast to view the architecture.
Get a drink at the Drake Hotel.
Eat at Chinatown.
Attend a dance at the Aragon Ballroom (if it opens).
Watch the Cubs lose at Wrigley Field.
Visit both the Field Museum and Museum of Science and Industry.
Drive in Chicago rush hour traffic.
Take the El.

The experience will make you appreciate major metropolitan living, as well as make you acutely aware of all its drawbacks.

(The Green Mill in Chicago. Best jazz in the town and a favorite hangout of Al Capone)

The Cheap Man's Reconnaissance

While it's recommended you approach becoming a Reconnaissance Man in an organized, methodical, and thorough manner, you may not simply have the time, money, or flexibility to do so. Expecting a 16 year old high school sophomore to fully explore all 16 reconnaissance states by the time he's 18, or a student debt-laden 22 year old to have the finances to last an entire summer in the field, is a tall order for anybody to fill. However, if you simply set out to see the "Must Visit" list in an abbreviated version of reconnaissance, chances are you'll achieve about 95% of what you need to in order to become a Reconnaissance Man. It might be a sleep-deprived-mad-dash across the country, and you may have to do it on a bare bones budget, but in simply seeing the greatest things this country has to offer it is almost a guarantee you will grow as an individual, find out more about yourself than you have the previous decade past, and come out of the journey with the knowledge and confidence of what you want to do in life.

The End

VISIT AARON'S WEBSITES!

Consulting
http://www.assholeconsulting.com

Podcast
http://www.soundcloud.com/aaron-clarey

Blog
http://captaincapitalism.blogspot.com

Books
http://www.amazon.com/Aaron-Clarey/e/B00J1ZC350/ref=sr_tc_2_0?qid=1412768111&sr=8-2-ent

YouTube
https://www.youtube.com/user/AaronClarey

Twitter
http://www.twitter.com/aaron_clarey

BOOKS BY AARON CLAREY

(Available in paperback, kindle, and some audiobooks on Amazon.com)

Curse of the High IQ

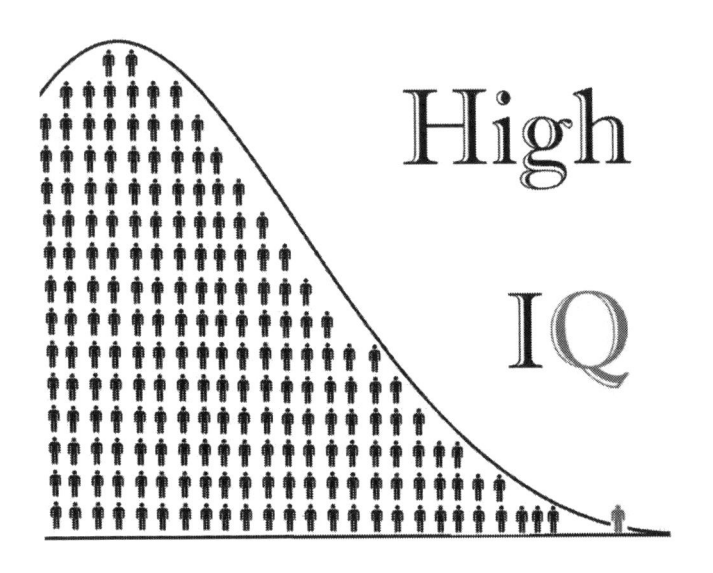

by
Aaron Clarey

Worthless

Copyright 2011

AMENTIBUS

The Young Person's Indispensable Guide to Choosing the Right Major

By
Aaron Clarey

ENJOY THE DECLINE

Accepting and Living with the Death of the United States

By
Aaron Clarey

The Black Man's Guide Out of Poverty

by
Aaron Clarey

Made in the USA
San Bernardino, CA
03 June 2018